Advance Praise for

Readin' + Writin' FOR THE Hard-Hat Crowd

"Susan R. Merrifield is one of a small group of researchers who has brought the lens of critical educational scholarship to the study of higher education. *Readin' and Writin' for the Hard-Hat Crowd* unpacks the linkages between liberal education, the urban university, and non-traditional students in a way that few studies have. The author has given us a masterful history of how faculty struggled over extending higher education to working-class students and the impact of that conflict on the development of this public university and its curriculum."

Barry M. Franklin, Professor and Department Head, Department of Secondary Education, Utah State University, Logan, Utah

"There is an element of Shakespearian tragedy in Susan R. Merrifield's wonderful account of one urban university's move from a clear, though probably misguided, effort to 'provide blue-collar college students with access to the cultural knowledge of the highly literate' (one that showed far too little respect for the cultural knowledge of the students it was recruiting), to a school too-often satisfied with a low standard of accomplishment. Yet there is also hope in her urgent plea that this society make a new—and as yet unheard of—commitment that links respect for student experience, high academic standards, and a significant new level of public investment in the hard-hat crowd who are our future."

James W. Fraser, Dean of the School of Education, Northeastern University, Boston, Massachusetts

Readin' + Writin' FOR THE Hard-Hat Crowd

HISTORY OF SCHOOLS & SCHOOLING

Alan R. Sadovnik and Susan F. Semel
General Editors

Vol. 21

PETER LANG
New York • Washington, D.C./Baltimore • Bern
Frankfurt am Main • Berlin • Brussels • Vienna • Oxford

Susan R. Merrifield

Readin' + Writin' FOR THE Hard-Hat Crowd

Curriculum Policy at an Urban University

PETER LANG
New York • Washington, D.C./Baltimore • Bern
Frankfurt am Main • Berlin • Brussels • Vienna • Oxford

Library of Congress Cataloging-in-Publication Data

Merrifield, Susan R.
Readin' and writin' for the hard-hat crowd /
Susan R. Merrifield.
p. cm. — (History of schools and schooling; vol. 21)
Includes bibliographical references.
1. English philology—Study and teaching—United States.
2. Working class—Education (Higher)—United States.
3. Nontraditional college students—United States.
4. Education, Urban—United States.
I. Title. II. Series: History of schools
and schooling; v. 21.
PE69.M37M47 420'.71'174461—dc21 00-066414
ISBN 0-8204-5508-3
ISSN 1089-0678

Bibliographic information published by **Die Deutsche Bibliothek**.
Die Deutsche Bibliothek lists this publication in the "Deutsche Nationalbibliografie"; detailed bibliographic data is available on the Internet at http://dnb.ddb.de/.

Cover photo by Bruce W. Roberts
Cover design by Lisa Barfield

Peter Lang Publishing, Inc., New York
275 Seventh Avenue, 28th Floor, New York, NY 10001
www.peterlangusa.com

To my inspiration
husband and daughter
Bruce and Margaret

And the teachers who nurtured our intelligence
With infinite gratitude

And
in honor and regret
to all women who sacrifice creativity and personal ambition
for what we have known as love

CONTENTS

AUTHOR'S NOTE

Urban State University is a pseudonym, as are the names of most people and places menioned in this study.

ACKNOWLEDGMENTS

To begin, I need to acknowledge just how difficult this process has been. In the twenty years that I have spent gathering information about the place I call Urban State University, I have met and received material from several scholars who once believed that they would write a similar history. Like pioneers who left behind beloved objects when the wagon train lightened its load, the books that lived inside the school's founding mothers and fathers were sacrificed to the interests of time, work, health, or family. My house and office are full of the collected papers of many people who have been associated with this university. To these friends and colleagues, I offer both my gratitude and the hope that this book in some way honors their careers. In particular, I wish to acknowledge the first dean of the College of Arts and Sciences who has graciously and generously offered me both hours of fascinating conversation and an example of a life dedicated to equitable public education.

This study evolved from research begun at the Harvard Graduate School of Education. Therefore, I wish to thank my committee; Marvin Lazerson, Barbara Newell and the late Paul Ylvisaker. The completion of that project was realized with the support of the Woodrow Wilson National Fellowship Foundation, which awarded me a Spencer Fellowship. More recently this study has been supported by the Russell Fellowship at Lesley University.

This book sits in your hands because of the thoughtfulness of Jim Fraser who introduced me to Chris Myers at Peter Lang. I appreciate both the patience and advice that Chris has offered me during the years that have passed since our introduction. Others at Lang, particularly Bernadette Shade and Lisa Dillon, have invested a great deal of time and expertise in the completion of the manuscript. The insights and suggestions of my series editor, Alan Sadovnik, have both enlightened and pushed me closer to this finish line.

A number of friends and colleagues read various chapters of the manuscript; their insights and advice were invaluable. I especially wish to recognize Carole Robinson, Barry Franklin, and my husband, Bruce Roberts.

I cannot thank enough those kind friends who supported me as I struggled to wrestle with formatting a book on my cranky eMac. In this regard, I must salute the tireless and generous support of Dave Powers at Lesley University. I also offer warmest appreciation to Lori Mandolese, Mike Wilander, and Barbara Ulm.

And finally I must both thank and honor the support and memory of my dear friend, the late Dr. Sally A. Lubeck. When my writing was finally "on a roll" in the fall of 2003, she suggested that we postpone a long anticipated visit until the summer. At the time, she was looking forward to reading *Hard Hat* and she thought that others were too. Her death in April cut short our summer plans. If I could take back time, I would go to Ann Arbor and spend a precious week with Sally; but since that's not how life works, I can only wish that this work in some way fulfills her belief in my ability to tell a good story.

July 2004

INTRODUCTION

READIN' AND WRITIN' FOR THE HARD-HAT CROWD: CURRICULUM POLICY AT AN URBAN UNIVERSITY

Looking backward is difficult. It is especially difficult when the subject of our recollections is one that played a central role in our lives. Remembering causes us to confront lost battles and dreams, as well as memories of past successes, accomplishments and discoveries; perhaps, we are even forced to confront the ghost of a younger, now strangely innocent self or time. As the first dean of the College of Arts and Sciences at Urban State University, Stephen Millet, told me, "I have resisted looking at the history of this institution—I don't think I could stand it."

Mine has not been dry research. Unearthing the facts, recollections, myths, and legends of four decades of curriculum development has drawn me close to vibrant personalities and exciting recent history. Since the 1960s, this country has experienced enormous social transformation and schools are among those institutions most affected by this change. As an institution born out of the social change of the 1960s, the history of this university has much to say to those who study higher education, particularly public higher education. Because U.S.U. has always been caught in verbal crossfire over what constitutes the best curricula for first-generation college students, this story should be important to those who are concerned about attracting, retaining, and understanding these undergraduates.

Throughout its history, Urban State University has served local low- and moderate-income students. Therefore, it is an example of an institution consistently grappling with the academic needs of nontraditional students with weak preparation for the liberal arts. While the history of Introductory English could once be understood to be the story of the college's response to the need to provide effective instruction in college-level reading and writing to this new population, by the late 1980s, this story was complicated by the fact that the majority of the graduates of Urban State completed Freshman English at another institution. Therefore, the university's introductory courses were no longer a foundation for the kind of four-year experience that the founding fathers had envisioned. By the beginning of the 21st century, with transfer students accounting for over 75 percent of the undergraduate population, the median age of students dropping, and a much debated student center and dormitories set for construction, many believed the college had turned its back on both its original mission and the commuter students it was founded to serve.

For almost two decades, I have listened to the voices of the faculty and administrators who played a significant role in the development and delivery of Introductory English instruction. This is hardly a subject all parties involved have agreed upon any more than it is a subject upon which policymakers and educational theorists agree. However, this complex story is particularly compelling to me, not only because my research and much of my teaching career has focused on the education of low-income students, but also because as a member of U.S.U.'s third class, I was part of that group of undergraduates referred to by the university's first chancellor as "the hard-hat crowd." A graduate of the class of 1971, I returned to my alma mater twice, in the mid-1970s and again in the 1980s as an instructor of Freshman English. Because I was a student when the majority of my classmates failed to perform at the standard set by the university's founding fathers, as an instructor, I was motivated to create a learning environment in which students could acquire proficiency in reading and writing, rather than experience more disappointment and failure. Both my successes and mistakes were illuminating, instilling in me a desire to look more deeply at the multitude of issues inherent in the education of underprepared college students.

In his *Handbook on Undergraduate Curriculum*, Arthur Levine notes: "A new college is the easiest way to establish a nontraditional mission or curriculum."[1] Certainly, in a state dominated by high quality private liberal arts colleges, establishing a state university for the purpose of providing a first rate curriculum in the Liberal Arts to local low-income residents was nontraditional, given that the state legislature modestly supported only a small state teacher's college in the metropolitan area.

However, as Levine also notes, "New schools rarely fulfill all of the expectations of their founders."[2] Dean Stephen Millet would be quick to agree. New schools, particularly state schools, are subject to so many external forces, which their founders may not understand or anticipate. The legislature, the general public, the quality of the local high schools, the financial climate, and many other factors affect the direction of academic programs.

The founders of U.S.U. wanted to offer an empowering curriculum to a new type of college student. In a sense, they wanted to do nothing less than expand the meaning of being human for this undergraduate population.

The history of the curriculum of Introductory English contains within in it an evolving conception of what should be taught to this new population as well as what could be taught, given the constraints of student preparedness, budgets, and faculty resources.

One thing is sure, the academic (as opposed to the political) founders of the university were very clear about what the primary mission of the new school should be:

> The first aim, of course, must be to build a university in the ancient tradition of Western civilization, to gather an academy of scholars devoted to intellectual freedom and integrity, to preserving and extending knowledge and wisdom while teaching both as well as they can.[3]

The first chairman of the English Department, Douglas Sheehan, agreed completely with the above mission statement and he was confident that it implied a need for a Great Books curriculum for Introductory English. Over the years, the mission of this much larger and multifaceted university has evolved, as has the curriculum of Introductory English. But, this should come as no surprise. At the beginning of any venture, as in a marriage, the right road to travel seems clear, even obvious. But things happen. Characters enter and leave and events occur over which we have no control. On their 30th anniversary, the couple bears little resemblance to the young innocents who walked down the aisle. Yet something of their original sentiment must remain or their marriage ceases to exist. Such is the case with U.S.U. and its Introductory English curriculum—they are both greatly changed. It is up to the reader to determine whether or not something of the school's original spirit and purpose still remains.

·1·

TO EXTEND THE MORRILL ACT, 1964–1965

Now we must seek out, and support, those young people whose race, or recent immigration, or depressed economic status, denies them higher education and even the expectation of it. Any state university that does not actively recruit the able children of the Negro, the Puerto Rican, the unskilled or migratory laborer, is not doing its job in the middle of the 20th century, is not bringing the Morrill Act up to date.

JUNE 1965
STATEMENT OF PURPOSE

Looking back almost forty years, some people involved with education in this region say that they recall a great deal of opposition to the creation of an urban branch of the state university; others recall it as an idea whose time had come. This had always been a place where the majority of college students were out-of-state residents attending private schools; the legislature was not used to spending much money on public higher education. As the sixties began, only 16 percent of in-state college students attended public institutions.[1] In fact, in 1964, the year in which U.S.U. was conceived, this state ranked 50th per capita in expenditures for public higher education.[2]

In 1987, the late Gerard Daley didn't recall that there had been much debate over the need for U.S.U. The former president of the state senate and self-proclaimed long-time friend of public higher education recalled that there was little deliberation over the topic once he and his colleagues decided that the state needed an urban public university.

On May 3, 1964, Daley picked the Newman Center at the flagship campus (State University) as the setting for his speech announcing enthusiastic support of the establishment of the new school. He knew that this would be no ordinary communion breakfast speech, which he usually gave to an exclusively Catholic audience who came to hear an inspiring religious theme from the senate president. No, this was to be an historic statement. Therefore, Daley recalled, asking a nearby state college president and old friend, Dr. Patrick O'Neil, to ghostwrite his speech. Said Daley, "What better place to call for the new campus than at the flagship campus where thousands of qualified applicants had been turned away."[3]

President Thomas of the flagship campus and other important university and state officials were present at that communion breakfast. The month before, the university president had reported to the Senate Ways and Means Committee, "that approximately 8,000 high school students seeking admission to the university's freshman class will be turned away."[4] Daley assumed that Thomas and others would get his message about the need for the urban site and support him. He was right. The next day, the president expressed agreement with Daley's agenda.[5]

According to Daley, very soon after that well attended breakfast at the Newman Center, he met with his friend Senator John Connors and told him that he was going to file a bill which he wanted to pass quickly; Connors agreed to co-sponsor the bill to authorize the creation of U.S.U. with Daley and they decided to get a young member of the house, James Riley, to sponsor the bill also.

Daley told a story that indicated very little opposition to the establishment of U.S.U. It seems that he thought that the metropolitan area needed a public liberal arts college and he simply marshaled his troops in the state legislature and got what he wanted. He dismissed opposition from a nearby large private university as inconsequential ("No one listened to them") and recalls that his only obstacle was the president of the city's only public teacher's college. However, newspaper clippings and other data from that period suggest that there was at least a substantial public dialogue about the desirability of an urban branch of the flagship campus.

All parties involved in the debate agreed there was, as one city newspaper stated, "an explosion" of baby boomers needing college education, particularly in the metropolitan areas. However, the appropriate response to this educational crisis was not clear. In 1964, the vast majority of postsecondary students in this state attended private colleges.[6] Hence, representatives of some private institutions anticipated and pressured the legislature and the general public for enhanced support of their institutions as the best solution to the need for expansion in higher education. But as Freeland notes in *Academia's Golden Age*, this pressure for public subsidies for private schools was not as strong as one might imagine because many of these schools had their sights set on attracting highly qualified out-of-state residents. From this perspective, many leaders of private colleges almost welcomed the prospect of the state responding to the needs of its rapidly expanding youth population.[7]

In a June 4, 1964 letter to alumni of the large private university mentioned above, its president asked that pressure be exerted on the legislature not to enact the bill that would establish another public university until a thorough review of relevant data was analyzed.[8] He asked that influence be generated to postpone the vote until a report which would evaluate the total educational needs and facilities in the state was completed and there was a full presentation of cost estimates and a decision reached as to the anticipated scope of future upper-division and graduate courses.

The leadership of both the local public teachers' college and this private university objected strenuously to the notion that the region needed a new public university with a liberal arts orientation. The president of the teacher's college, Dr. Garrity, made it clear to Gerard Daley that he believed that his institution provided the answer to the state's educational crisis. (He must have also felt threatened by the prospect of a second public college so close to his own. Such fears would be justified, for in the early 1980s, this campus was forced to merge with Urban State by the newly created Board of Regents.) Garrity argued that it made much more sense to enhance the Liberal Arts component of his teacher-training program than to start from scratch with a new, very expensive institution.[9]

Representatives from both private and public schools maintained that tax dollars could be saved and the interests of students better served by drawing upon and expanding the resources of existing local institutions. For many in state government, this argument held little weight, as the proposed new school, viewed as a satellite of State University, would be part of an institution with the highest caliber of academic programming of any state school.

The representatives of the various schools that opposed the establishment of U.S.U. would continue to play a role in the life of this public institution but they were unsuccessful in their attempts to block its establishment. In 1964, as Daley had anticipated, the state legislature was moved to action when the flagship campus received 12,000 applications for 2,600 places in the freshman class of '65–66. Given that the greatest percentage of these applicants came from the urban area,[10] the legislature was being asked to bring the land-grant university into the twentieth century by authorizing a campus in one of the state's largest cities. Proponents of the urban site had successfully argued that the rural populations which the Morrill Act had originally served by providing agricultural and mechanical education were now part of the middle class. Therefore, the 20th-century goal of this 19th-century legislation was to benefit those urban residents still left out of the educational pipeline by virtue of race, recent immigration, or income.[11]

The senate bill that provided for the establishment of Urban State University came before the Joint Committee on Education on May 27, 1964. The president of the flagship campus addressed the committee. He asked that they not wait for the results of further study of the issue, but move quickly so that 1,000 students might enter the new school in the fall of 1965. He pleaded that too many qualified residents would miss out on the chance of a college education if action was delayed:

> There is no question about the need to extend our resources for the benefit of the state's young people. There is no state in the Union that depends so much on a continuing flow of well-educated people as this one. Its vastly increasing space-age industry is only one example of a total enterprise that will demand more and more brainpower as we move toward the 21st century, now only about 36 years away and well within the life span of the students we are educating today.[12]

By June 18, 1964, the act had been signed by both the Acting Speaker of the House of Representatives and Gerard Daley, president of the senate, as well as Governor Edmund Winslow. Under the legislation an initial appropriation of $200,000 was granted for planning the university.[13]

Somehow, within 14 months, a new public university had to be created. President Thomas named a four-man task force to prepare and refine plans for the university. Speaking on July 9, 1964, Thomas said: "We intend to accept 1,000 students by the fall of 1965. This means that courses must be formulated, faculty must be hired, budgets must be prepared, admissions procedures must be established, catalogs will have to be printed, and adequate facilities will have to be found—all in the next few months."[14]

The management consultant firm of Wilfred Dowson Associates took on the task of studying and making site recommendations. In November 1964, the architectural and engineering firm of Drummond and Smith was hired to make cost studies of sites recommended by Dowson Associates. The site selected, The Old Electric Company Building, was located in the heart of the city.

On February 12, 1965, Dr. James W. Dooley, academic vice president at a large southwestern state university was named the first chancellor. Dooley had been an administrator at the flagship campus prior to his appointment in the southwest. Gerard Daley, speaking of his former colleagues in the state legislature, recalled "everyone loved Jim."[15] At that time, Daley felt that Dooley's popularity would be enough to get him the financial support he would require. According to him, stingy allocations from the flagship campus, and not lack of support from the legislature, turned out to be the thorn in Chancellor Dooley's side.

In January of that year, Dr. Stephen Millet of the History Department at the flagship campus and Dr. Edward Gallant of its Botany Department were authorized to begin a national search for faculty. At one point in the planning stage, there was a proposal to have six small liberal arts colleges at the city campus. However, according to one former U.S.U. administrator, "this idea died aborning"; hence, Millet and Gallant were charged with the task of selecting faculty for only one college.[16] They received over 600 inquiries from professors who were attracted to the location and the opportunity to be part of a new beginning.[17]

State University's then Chancellor Caruso recruited a friend from his undergraduate days to the new school; he gave Douglas Sheehan his pick of positions. Professor Sheehan chose to be the head of Humanities, simultaneously becoming the first chairman of the English Department.[18] As chairman of Notre Dame's English Department, Caruso's college friend was well qualified for both positions.

Sheehan became Millet's partner in the development of the first Humanities faculty and curriculum. No stranger to this state's system of higher education, Sheehan had attended the flagship campus as an undergraduate and at the age of 35 became a full professor at a suburban satellite campus where he taught returning veterans from 1946–49.[19]

Sheehan's hiring and recruitment practices had a profound effect on the English Department well into the last years of the twentieth century. At Notre Dame, he had the opportunity to meet many new PhDs whose educational philosophies were congenial with his own. For example, in 1964, Sheehan interviewed Richard Clover for a vacancy in the department. Impressed with Clover's enthusiasm for the classics, he invited him to join the new faculty in 1965.[20]

Sheehan and Millet shared many perspectives on the undergraduate curriculum, including a belief that students ought to be exposed to classical literature early in their college careers. History would give mixed reviews of the Great Books curriculum they developed in 1965. Some of their critics, both on and off campus, would accuse these men of betraying the dreams of local working class students by their elitist attitudes toward curriculum. However, Millet and Sheehan saw themselves as the architects of an experiment in a genuinely democratic form of general education. They believed that they were extending the mission of the Morrill Act to include the provision of an academic program strong enough to create access to middle class culture, values, and professions for the graduates of the local public schools. As late as 2002, Stephen Millet remained passionately committed to the belief that in a democratic society all students should be expected to achieve a high standard of content knowledge in the arts and sciences, not unlike the standards reached by the majority of students in Europe and parts of Asia.[21]

Ironically, by invoking the Morrill Act in their statement of purpose, the founding fathers introduced a symbol of conflict over curriculum that has been part of the fabric of this urban university since its beginning. As Kerr notes, when Abraham Lincoln signed the act in 1862, he was responding to "a growing democratic, even egalitarian and populist, trend in the nation."[22] As we know, a civil war was fought, at least in part, over the meaning of the word, "egalitarian." One hundred years after the enactment of this landmark legislation, a war of words was about to be waged over the content of curriculum at this university which was founded to bring "the Morrill Act up to date."

Most educational historians agree that there has always been wide disagreement about the sort of curriculum that should be delivered at land-grant universities.[23] This first federal legislation of its type moved American higher education far beyond its earlier role as preparation for the ministry, education, medicine, or law. Like Millet and Sheehan, there were some 19th century academics who believed that the Morrill Act meant the spread of classical studies, while others believed that the legislation mandated the sort of studies that would teach future farmers what "to do about hog cholera."[24] For almost a century and a half, impassioned disagreements have centered on whether or not poetry and philosophy are a waste of precious time or ennobling study for a class of people who need to learn how to view events from multiple perspectives.

In the 1860s, the young nation was experiencing agricultural and industrial expansion similar to the technological boom of the 1960s. In both historical periods, new populations had to be professionalized, and theories abounded as to how best to provide these new students with a college education that was liberal, yet served practical purposes. In both eras, the issue at hand was no less than the very nature of schooling in a democracy.

·2·

A WORKING CLASS HARVARD, 1965

The right to culture is also a right of the person—and only if we believe in the value and dignity of the person can we believe also in the necessity for democracy.

STEPHEN MILLET

Stephen Millet was eager to leave the History Department of State University in order to organize the new Humanities Division at U.S.U. He was fed up with the direction the flagship campus was moving in, which he characterized as, "expanding graduate programs without adding new faculty positions that would be required if one wanted to continue to do both jobs well."[1] (The two jobs were, of course, teaching undergraduates and teaching graduate students.) At S.U., he was required to teach introductory lectures to a hundred or more students without the support of what he considered adequate assistance. He was excited by the possibility of moving away from what he perceived as a national trend toward "image flexing" through the development of redundant graduate programs.

His plans for the new Humanities Division included a reversal of the traditional class size arrangements in higher education. He envisioned small, intimate seminar-type classes for freshmen and sophomores that would facilitate the special attention that underprepared college students would require. As Levine states, "Compensatory education in particular seeks by enrichment to overcome deprivations associated with the home, family, and earlier study."[2] In this regard, Millet's goal was to replicate the freshman seminar as introduced by Nathan Pusey at Lawrence College in 1945, which emphasized general education in an intimate setting as a means of moving away from the traditional large lecture halls of earlier eras.[3] In small classes headed by first-rate faculty, Millet envisioned that underprepared but motivated students would receive instruction and practice in reading and writing in all classes, not just English courses.[4]

While on sabbatical, Millet stayed in the home of an old friend who lived near the site of the urban campus. Meeting frequently over coffee with this well known scholar of higher education and Doug Sheehan, the trio created a coherent curriculum package which covered over twenty centuries of Western literature and history during four semesters. By July of 1965, they had developed an interdisciplinary syllabus for the Humanities (Figure 1), which offered first-year students an extensive introduction to Western culture.

Over two decades after it was developed, Douglas Sheehan could still respond to this curriculum as if it were a new idea, rather than a series of literary works he was first introduced to over sixty years earlier. Speaking in the late 1980s, he was quick to point out that although this syllabus came to be known as "the Great Books," it would have been more appropriate to consider it an introduction to world literature because the Great Books, as they were studied at St. John's University, were a collection of over one hundred texts which included scientific literature.[6]

During a 1987 interview, Stephen Millet also appeared alive with memories. Glancing up from a copy of the original 1965 syllabus, he recalled that the mid-sixties preceded "the activist explosion." Said Miller, "We were very innocent. We were still operating under old assumptions."[7] According to him, faculty were excited by the two-year curriculum which combined the study of the Great Books with the study of Western civilization. Millet remembered that job interviews were full of favorable comments about the literature and many people were recruited for their experience with similar curricula.

One can certainly question whether or not Millet is accurate in his assessment that 1965 was "before the activist explosion." The Free Speech movement had already begun. Bob Dylan had already told the nation that "The times they are a-changin'," and very significant Civil Rights activism had been underway for almost a decade, culminating in the passage of major Civil Rights legislation in 1964. Even Millet's own rhetoric in a July 1965 statement of purpose indicates a significant level of social awareness: "Who among us will have nothing to do about poverty, crime, apathy, ignorance, ugliness and decay? About human degradation, humiliation and isolation? This is the hard, demanding side of this new university."[8]

During the 1960s, much of the focus of the War on Poverty involved using public education as a means of creating equal opportunity. With this in mind, it seems that Millet and Sheehan may have been just a little too innocent as they designed the Humanities curriculum for the fall of 1965. Millet has long claimed that in a true democracy, ordinary citizens must have access to a first rate education. Yet he should have been aware by the mid-sixties that requiring a rigorous traditional curriculum at an almost open admissions school would create yet another barrier for underprepared low-income

FIGURE 1 Proposed Syllabus for Coordinated English-History Program, Freshman Year

ENGLISH I	HISTORY I
Unit I. The Greek and Hebraic Tradition	
Sept. 15–Oct. 7 *Old Testament* Genesis: Stress on literary style and imagery: The Joseph Story, etc. Exodus Judges Ruth Amos Psalms Job Song of Solomon Ecclesiastes	Genesis: Stress on History Exodus I & II Samuel I Kings Isaiah
Oct. 8–Oct. 18 Homer, *The Odyssey*	History of Homeric Age
Oct. 20–Nov. 1 Greek Theater: *Agamemmon, Oedipus Rex, Frogs* or *Lysistrata* Selections from Aristotle's *Poetics*	4th & 5th C: Thucydides
Nov. 3–Nov. 13 Plato: *Ion, Euthyphro*	*Apology, Crito, Republic*
Unit II. Late Classical & Early Christian	
Nov. 15–Nov. 24 Gospel of St. Luke St. Augustine's *Confessions* (Bks. 1,3,4,9)	St. Paul's First Epistle to the Corinthians St. Augustine's *City of God* (excerpts)
Unit III. The Medieval Period	
Nov. 25–Dec. 4 Malory, *Mort D'Arthur* (in 1 vol. collection) Chaucer, Prologue & One Tale Dante's *Inferno*	Feudal Society & Chivalry *Song of Roland* *Little Flowers of St. Francis*
Unit IV. The Renaissance	
Dec. 6–Dec. 18 Marlowe's *Dr. Faustus* Shakespeare's *Henry IV*	Machiavelli's *The Prince* Milton, *Areopagitica*
Jan. 3–Jan. 13 Renaissance Lyric Poetry	

FIGURE 1 *continued*

ENGLISH II	HISTORY II
Unit V. The Neo-Classical Age	
Feb. 3–Mar. 3	
Milton, *Samson Agonisten*	Voltaire, *Candide*
Moliere, *Tartuffe*	
Pope, *Rape of the Lock*	
Fielding, *Tom Jones*	
Unit VI. Romanticism and Revolution	
Mar. 4–Mar. 31	
Rousseau, *Confessions* (selections)	Rousseau, *Social Contract*
Wordsworth, *Prelude*, Bks. I, IX, & XII	Burke, *Reflections*
"Tintern Abbey"	Dickens, *Hard Times* or
Coleridge, "The Rime of the	Hammord's *Town*
Ancient Mariner"	*Laborers*
Keats, "St. Agnes Eve"	
"Ode on a Grecian Urn"	
Bronte, *Wuthering Heights*	
Thoreau, *Walden* (in part)	
Hawthorne, *Ethan Brand*	
Melville, *Billy Budd*	
Unit VII. Realism	
Apr. 1–Apr. 22	
Twain, *Huckleberry Finn*	
Dostoevsky, *Crime and Punishment*	
Tolstoy, *Death of Ivan Ilyich*	
Chekov, *The Kiss*	
Unit VIII. The Twentieth Century	
Apr. 23–May 25	
Conrad, *Heart of Darkness*	Remarque, *All Quiet on*
Joyce, *Portrait of the Artist as*	*the Western Front*
a Young Man	Koestler, *Darkness at*
Kafka, *Metamorphosis*	*Noon*
Eliot, *Murder in the Cathedral*	
Faulkner, *The Bear*	
Warren, *All The King's Men*	
Selected readings from Modern Poetry,	
ed. Mack, Dean and Frost (Prentice-Hall)[5]	

and minority students which many observers and participants might consider discriminatory.

One also wonders whether the newly hired, mostly left-leaning young faculty members were really as enthusiastic about the Great Books as Millet and Sheehan remembered. Perhaps they were only enthusiastic about being hired. More likely, their excitement was primarily generated by the often mentioned prospect of teaching students who were "truly working-class." Many of the new faculty had already taught less traditional introductory English curricula at other schools; this may have caused them to be reluctant to try something new, or old, as the case might be.

Perhaps even Sheehan and Millet had second thoughts about the rigor of their curriculum. By the end of the summer of '65, they decided that only a few pilot sections of the original interdisciplinary syllabus would be taught. The syllabus presented to the new English faculty in September 1965 was somewhat modified from the July version. Basically, a few texts were eliminated or became optional and the interdisciplinary component was eliminated in all but a few sections.[9]

Even though their introductory Humanities curriculum was all but completely dismantled by 1971, Millet and Sheehan maintained their belief in this sort of undergraduate education throughout the twentieth century. Although Sheehan died in the late 1990s, Stephen Millet is still actively engaged in the development of national standards that are consistent with those inherent in the curriculum once taught to the hard-hat crowd.[10] As he told me somewhat defiantly in 2003, "My attitude toward curriculum remains basically unchanged. I still have an axe to grind."[11]

Millet's educational philosophy was heavily influenced by the 1945 Harvard "Redbook," while Sheehan's philosophy was inspired by studying with Norman Foerster who was the head of the School of Letters at Iowa when he worked toward his doctorate. In Foerster's *The American State University: The Relation to Democracy* written in 1937, he argues that state universities have failed when they only prepare youth for work, rather than the sort of enlightened citizenship that a free society requires.[12] Foerster frequently finds support for his educational philosophy in the words of Thomas Jefferson who believed that public universities should offer "liberal education worthy to receive, and able to guard the sacred deposits of the rights and liberties of their fellow citizens."[13] Similarly, the "Redbook" advocates that general education for underclassmen should be distinct from education for specialization.[14] Jefferson, Foerster, the authors of the "Redbook," Millet and Sheehan are all in agreement that an ennobling, intellectually empowering education ought to be available to all who are capable, as Thomas Jefferson advocated, "without regard to wealth, birth, or other accidental condition or circumstance."[15]

It is difficult to criticize the spirit that motivated these founding fathers when it is an expression of the premise that if a particular form of education is good enough for the rich, it's good enough for the poor. If they are to be criticized at all, it is for being too naive or innocent, as Millet claimed. In retrospect, it appears that while Sheehan and Millet fully understood that early specialization can be a form of job training rather than genuine liberal education, they did not completely understand the student population for whom they were developing curricula or the environment in which they were operating. In particular, Sheehan seems to have thought that U.S.U. students would be similar to the returning World War II veterans to whom he taught classic literature in the late 1940s. This misconception may have been the factor that caused them to neglect two important, if not poignant, realities affecting curriculum at the urban campus—the influence of the local private colleges and the flagship campus and the intellectual isolation of low-income commuter students.

Many of the private colleges in the area offered a first rate education in the liberal arts. As the first dean of the College of Arts and Sciences, Millet should have realized that the administrators at many area private colleges would pressure the state legislature to back away from subsidizing a high quality public version of their kind of curriculum. Sheehan, who had recently spent many years in a well-funded state system, may not have been fully aware of the power of the private sector but Millet, as a professor at State University and a product of local public schools and colleges, should have realized the potential for opposition to an almost free traditional liberal arts program in the metropolitan area.

Likewise, it seems odd that the founding fathers did not consider the effect that the student population's lifestyle and educational background would have on their capacity to pursue an elite form of education. These were not students living a collegiate lifestyle; these were working class people attending a commuter college. Much of the early U.S.U. rhetoric acknowledges this fact with a pride that borders on glamorizing the university's working class heroes. ("You are not the beanie-bedecked fledglings dotting a thousand campuses throughout the land this September; you wear 'hard hats' as the student body of a new adventurous University with an urgent, compelling job to do."[16]) But, it seems that little energy was invested in thinking through what this would actually mean in terms of instruction and curriculum.

Certainly, Foerster and many other educational theorists who concern themselves with public higher education shy away from this issue. They tell us what first generation college students should learn in order to rise to the level of their more privileged peers; but, for the most part, they avoid the issue of the myriad effects of the frequent shortage of space and time to reflect and study in the lives of working commuter students. Residential campus life may have its barriers to study; a student may have to struggle to find a quiet corner to study on a Saturday night. But, there is always the library, just minutes away from the dorm. While it is true that the children of immigrants who attended CCNY in the early part of the 20th century often lived in circumstances more sparse than those inhabited by the "hard-hat crowd," they usually came from families with a single-minded commitment to "the right to culture." Traub describes first generation tenement dwellers who structured their lives around and concentrated their limited resources on the college education of one of their sons.[17] These immigrant parents feverently believed that scholarship was a ticket out of poverty. In contrast, the vast majority of students in the first classes at U.S.U. lived lives that were not intended to promote study or solitude; most of my peers simply continued the lives they led before they entered college and somehow tried to "fit college in." They often found themselves alone at 10 p.m. with their books and assignments—isolated from the stimulation and support that students can receive from peers at a residential college. The student's family generally could not provide him with a conversation about *The Divine Comedy*, or even an expression of belief that the acquisition of this knowledge was important.

The class of '69 at Urban State University consisted mostly of working class people who usually worked over 30 hours a week in order to attain a college education in a few, elderly, dilapidated buildings in the city's Garden Square. The students, most of whom were at least somewhat older than the traditional 18, would commute home at the end of a long day to lay down their copies of Virgil, Homer, and *Introduction to Biology* in triple deckers located in neighborhoods on the city's margins.

On the East coast, this "hard-hat crowd" was an entirely new type of public university student. Within five years, faculty at the long renowned City College of New York would meet a similar population.[18]

Most English faculty say they became aware quickly that many of their students simply did not have time in their busy lives to read one lengthy and challenging literary work per week. Hence, present and former faculty often cite student schedules and limited secondary education as reasons why they pressured the department to abbreviate the Introductory English curriculum during the sixties. However, Millet and Sheehan remained resolute about the curriculum in the face of such opposition. They both felt that small class size would serve sufficiently to compensate for the isolation common to commuter students, as well as the need for academic support. Millet claims that he always realized that many U.S.U. students would be unable to successfully complete the rigorous core course requirements. He viewed the school's mission as providing equal opportunity to an elite form of education—not guaranteeing a degree to all who entered.

Millet's philosophy is in line with that of Thomas Jefferson, founder of one of the nation's first state universities, who saw the primary mission of public higher education as developing the natural intellectual aristocrats among the lower classes. While it is true that some U.S.U. students did survive academically in spite of poor high school preparation, work schedules, family demands and cramped apartments, the values of the sixties made this running-the-gauntlet approach to public higher education unattractive, if not unconscionable, to many faculty whose concern for their students was often motivated by political and personal values that caused them to see the potential in students who did not experience success with the original curriculum.

This conflict over curriculum was yet another expression of the contradictions inherent in the language Dean Millet used to describe and promote the general education program of 1965. He employed the language and ideals of the War on Poverty and the Morrill Act to advance a Jeffersonian conception of public higher education. In the reality of gritty classrooms, it would prove difficult to both offer equal opportunity to the hard-hat crowd and nurture the best and the brightest among the city's poor.

·3·

NOTHING BUT THE FUTURE: THE GREAT BOOKS, THE HARD-HAT CROWD, AND THE SIXTIES, 1965–1969

"I think you deserve the hard hat; you don't look like a beanie crowd to me."
CHANCELLOR JAMES W. DOOLEY
SEPTEMBER 1965

In September 1965, Urban State University opened its doors to 1,242 students.[1] Dean Millet had originally hoped that the first class would consist of no more than 800 students.[2] However, there was enormous political pressure on the state system to justify the creation of the new campus. That first year, admissions were controlled by the flagship campus, which felt a big need to show overenrollment figures to the legislature as well as the taxpayers. Hence, 75 percent of the applicants to the new school were accepted.[3]

In retrospect, Millet now sees serious problems with the 1965 admission policy. He envisioned, "a first rate public college for the able students of the area."[4] But the admissions office at the flagship campus accepted many students who were less than able to take on the academic demands of a rigorous liberal arts program.[5] In the late 1980s, Millet expressed regret that these underprepared students were never interviewed in order to determine whether they had the determination, intelligence, and energy to persist in spite of their limited preparation for college work.

Although he had no control over the general admissions process in 1965, Millet did develop and administer a small, experimental program designed to bring nontraditional, very low income, older students into the new urban university. Most of these students did not satisfy the minimum requirements of regular admissions (SAT and Achievement scores and graduation from an accredited college preparatory high school program).

Millet ran the Special Admissions program as he wished all of the admissions process ran. This program consisted of both outreach to the community (public school personnel, parole officers, clergy, social workers, etc.) for the purpose of recruitment and individual interviews for candidates. Recruitment and interviews were conducted to find underprepared mostly minority students who had the will and the intelligence to work hard and succeed, in spite of the gaps in their previous educational experiences. Had this model been in place for all applicants, the first freshman class most likely would have been smaller, but more capable of persistence.

At the first faculty and student convocation on September 23, 1965, Chancellor James W. Dooley was emphatic about the mission of the new university: "the first aim of Urban State University, of course, must be to build a university in the ancient tradition of Western civilization, to gather an academy of scholars devoted to intellectual freedom and integrity, to preserving and extending knowledge and wisdom while teaching both as well as they can. Anything that detracts from or delays this fundamental work of a university must be regarded as secondary to our main mission or even inimical to all our aims. Our core must be sound."[6]

Taken literally, the "core" of which Chancellor Dooley spoke was the rigorous set of Core Course requirements that were instituted in an effort to transfer "the ancient traditions of Western Civilization" to the inner-city college students attending U.S.U. These requirements consisted of: four terms of English, four semesters of a foreign language, two semesters of Western Civilization, two semesters of Social Science, four terms of a natural science or math, and upper division distribution requirements of four terms outside the major division (two courses being above the introductory level, and done in Humanities).[7]

In 1965, the freshmen, who attended classes in the old Electric Building, took an Introductory English course which was designed to give them an overview of the literary canon of Western civilization, from Homer's *Odyssey* and Virgil's *Aeneid* in the fall to the work of Joyce, Faulkner and Yeats in the spring. According to Millet, the university's founding fathers were trying to create an undergraduate educational experience not much different from that offered at City College of New York during the 1940s and 50s. Of that experience, one student, Morris Freedman writes:

> My years as a student at City College seemed to offer me a rare chance to learn languages, read remote literature, sense other times, other qualities of life, ruminate about other value systems, discover the range of experience. . . . It must

> have been around my junior year that I began to hope I might, on the basis of my college education, use reading, writing, thinking, and talking—the process of learning—in some direct way to support myself in this world in these times. I count myself singularly fortunate in working out some degree of harmony between what I wanted to do and what I had to do. Those undergraduate days at CCNY established the basis for my way of life.[8]

The original mission of Urban State University was to offer capable, mostly disadvantaged students the same opportunity for a liberal education that Freedman received at CCNY. The author of U.S.U.'s original mission statement, Dean Millet, believed that the university should provide education in three categories: (1) education for a profession, (2) education for citizenship and, (3) education for self-realization and cultural enrichment.[9] He and Douglas Sheehan believed that the Great Books curriculum was needed as preparation for a full range of professions, education for citizenship, and cultural enrichment.

The creation of equal opportunity through public higher education was indeed the mission of City College for over one hundred years since its founding in 1847. In *City on a Hill*, Traub describes a public college that was a gateway to the American dream for the able sons of recent immigrants.[10] During the first half of the twentieth century, CCNY alumni consisted of the second highest number of PhDs in the nation, over a half dozen Nobel Prize winners, and numerous doctors, lawyers, accountants, engineers, educators, and other highly regarded professionals.[11] However, there is a critical difference between that institution at that time and U.S.U. during the mid-1960s. CCNY had stiff entrance requirements; students had to be well prepared for college work in order to gain admission. CCNY was "a place for motivated achievers seeking a ticket out of poverty."[12] In fact, by the late 1950s, only 13 percent of high school graduates in New York were able to gain admission to a city college.[13]

In contrast, the high school backgrounds of U.S.U.'s class of '69 were very uneven. With 24 percent of the students in the freshman class who took the test scoring between 450 and 350 on the Verbal SAT, one could easily predict that many would have great difficulty with college level English courses.[14] However, this seems to be the type of student Dean Millet anticipated. In a 1987 interview, he indicated that he did not expect that the bulk of the first class would have attended a college preparatory program in high school. Nonetheless, he prescribed traditional general education taught in small classes as the way for these underprepared students to catch up to their more privileged peers. It was not his intention that all who entered would be able to run the gauntlet—he only wanted to provide equal access ("more than once if necessary") to the race. In this regard, Millet's philosophy is consistent with

Sadovnik's[15] perspective on compensatory higher education that integrates or mainstreams underprepared students into traditional or regular college courses without specialized remediation; only the qualified among non-elites are allowed to continue with their college education. According to more egalitarian understandings of the purposes of compensatory education, this sink or swim approach is a form of elitism in itself.[16]

In the development of curricula, Millet seems to have been guided by his perspective as a historian. He did not believe that students could be truly educated until they had a thorough understanding of their cultural heritage. Hence, his priority for students was learning history, or more accurately, acquiring a historical perspective that included a background in world literature. Because of this orientation, "Millet's curriculum" (as it is called by English faculty, rather than "Sheehan's curriculum") was bound to meet with opposition from English Department faculty who were trained to value literature and composition as opposed to history, even though many of them recall personally liking the curriculum at first, "because, after all, it was literature."[17]

During the early years of U.S.U., the conflicts that developed over curriculum in no way appear to have extinguished enthusiasm and interest in the instruction of Introductory English. On the contrary, the heated discussions that occurred appeared to stimulate involvement. After all, during 1965–67, when there was only a freshmen and sophomore class, faculty only taught introductory courses. David Fields still recalls the "missionary feeling" that he and most faculty felt.[18] According to him, everyone knew there would be "a lot of sweat and journeyman work" involved in setting up curricula in a university that didn't have a library and was housed in a few old, dusty buildings. But the youthful faculty were, for the most part, already caught up in the rhetoric and ideals of both the War on Poverty and the anti-war movement. Therefore, many were eager to take the professional risk of building a career at this new urban university. The few older or more established academics who were drawn to U.S.U. were usually, like Robert Campbell and Bob Cooper, drawn to the possibilities of establishing new graduate programs.

Many refer to these early years as a time of "creative chaos."[19] People did not simply moan and groan about the problems they had with the Great Books curriculum; they went to work developing both revisions of the Great Books curriculum and new approaches to the instruction of Introductory English. Between 1967 and 1970, almost all full-time English faculty presented their version of the best curriculum to the department for consideration and review. Looking back, more than one professor found it rather ironic that this supposedly radical department was so completely engaged in the conservative task of finding the one right curriculum. Said Elizabeth Curtis in 1987: "It's hard to believe that we really thought there could be such a thing as the right curriculum."[20]

During this period, the amount of time, thought and attention given to development and enhancement of Introductory English by full-time faculty was astounding and not to be repeated after 1971 when most introductory courses were turned over to part-time adjuncts, and later graduate student interns. This combined with the fact that faculty were intellectually stimulated by their involvement with the creation of a new university led to almost constant tinkering with the curriculum of Introductory English.

Most faculty mention that they felt challenged by the opportunity to work with new kinds of college students; minorities, older students, and underprepared high school graduates. During this period when faculty were dedicating so much of their energies to teaching, many established lifelong friendships with students in the first classes. Therefore, recollections of how interesting and unique these few students were come easily. Over 20 years later, Will Clarke could still clearly and fondly recall a few days spent in a seacoast art community with faculty and students who were funded by Dean Millet to see a production of *A Long Day's Journey Into Night* and hold a seminar on the work of O'Neill. Clarke long maintained contact with students who went on that field trip.[21] Over 30 years later, a retired Zack Joplin remembers well the student who told him that he finished reading *The Brothers Karamzov* at three in the morning, and wanted to wake up all his friends and tell them about it. According to Joplin, the image of that working-class student wide awake with excitement over the discovery of the transformational power of a great writer symbolizes why he made his career at U.S.U. from 1968–2000.[22] This, he told me, more than anything else is "the legend" of the school, "that our mission was something essentially working class."

Faculty recollections of the remainder of the student body during the early years are much more vague and general. One gets the impression that the hard-hat crowd was a varied group, much more varied than one would typically find at most colleges. A picture emerges from faculty interviews of a top group of students who could compete successfully with college students at any school. This group included those students who became friends of faculty. Most faculty also describe a middle group of students who were similar to average students at other larger state universities. It is the bottom quarter of students who are described by many faculty as different from college students encountered previously. Several faculty mention a group of students in the first classes who were more needy, both academically and emotionally, than any undergraduates they have since encountered. Other faculty recollect students who were "astoundingly ill-prepared" and sometimes functionally illiterate. However, professors with previous experience at other small, less competitive state schools, such as Elizabeth Curtis's experience at Missouri State Teachers College, observe that their former students were quite similar to those at

U.S.U. On the other hand, faculty who had taught mostly at competitive private colleges viewed the majority of U.S.U. students as functioning academically on a level appropriate for community or junior college students. One such professor went so far as to describe U.S.U. in the mid-sixties as "a grade D community college."

While opinions vary as to the abilities of U.S.U. students during the sixties, it seems safe to say that any given Introductory English class had a wider range of student abilities than one generally found in most college classrooms. Some people believe that the low ability group was mostly composed of Special Admissions students who were admitted as early as 1965. There is no accurate data to tell us who the weakest students were but it seems safe to assume that since there weren't any remedial English courses until 1970, some of the seriously underprepared students that faculty speak of were Special Admissions students who were integrated into the regular Introductory English classes. However, it is important to note that Stephen Millet only admitted 25 students through Special Admission for the 1965–66 academic year. Special Admissions students did not comprise over 10 percent of the student body until 1971.[23]

Many faculty speak of receiving papers which were too incomprehensible to respond to during their first semester at U.S.U. Others cite examples of astoundingly low levels of preparation for college work, such as a student who asked one professor for a translation of Shakespeare.[24]

Dr. Sheehan received many complaints from faculty but he remained unconvinced that the curriculum should be changed. Some of Sheehan's reluctance to waiver from his original curriculum package may have been a function of the fact that he did not teach at all during that first year. His administrative responsibilities as chairman and head of the Humanities Division kept him out of the classroom. However, it seems unlikely that direct classroom experience would have changed his attitude much as his experience teaching English 111 and English 112 during 1966–67 did not cause him to initiate curriculum reform.

Douglas Sheehan's belief in the Great Books curriculum had been well established over thirty years before he came to Urban State University. In 1937, he rebelliously left the graduate program at Harvard to go to the Department of Letters at the University of Iowa. There, under the direction of Norman Foerster, faculty taught a carefully structured Great Books curriculum.

By the time he came to U.S.U., Sheehan had been working with the Great Books successfully for over 30 years at schools such as Princeton and Notre Dame. These experiences caused him to believe "that certain studies are more valuable than others."[25] This is probably the reason why he was not responsive to initial requests for a more abbreviated, contemporary, and relevant curriculum. Some faculty mention that they were so troubled by what they perceived to be Sheehan's dictatorial style and old-fashioned notions of curricula that they would not have stayed at U.S.U. if it looked as though he would continue to control the department. However, by the late sixties, with the arrival of powerful personalities such as Robert Campbell and Joe Caulfield, it became apparent that Dr. Sheehan would not be in charge for long.

Although Sheehan was very excited about bringing the Great Books to U.S.U., younger men such as David Fields, Bruce Hamilton, and Bob Cooper saw this curriculum as passe. It wasn't what they were teaching in Introductory English before they came to Urban State and it wasn't what they thought should be taught to college freshmen, particularly underprepared freshmen. It was their belief that the emphasis on dense, demanding texts got in the way of instruction in composition. Perhaps because they were of a generation which had just begun to devote serious scholarly attention to the development of composition theory, these men were full of innovative ideas about how writing skills should be taught. The implementation of these innovations was hindered by their obligation to teach the mandated syllabus.

The first faculty efforts at carving out more time for writing instruction centered on reducing the number of texts per course. By April of 1966, a lengthy memo from the Freshman Committee Chairman, Ian O'Malley, indicates that there would be a reduction in the number of texts assigned for the fall of 1966. ("A reduction in the amount of literature requiring class discussion is intended to increase the time needed for instruction in composition.") This memo also requests that faculty submit the titles of books that they would like to see deleted or added to the syllabus. O'Malley emphasized: "In considering the entire syllabus, please note an important difference from the one we have worked with this year. Considerable latitude in substituting titles has been expected and has occurred."[26]

O'Malley's 1966 memo reveals some erosion of Sheehan's authority over curriculum. More important, this document states that by the second year of operations, a larger portion of instructional time was to be given to the instruction of composition, rather than literary analysis.

The issues covered in O'Malley's memo were not the only subjects about which faculty complained. Dr. Fields recalls that he was particularly troubled by the lack of standards for assignments. Although departmental memoranda from the mid-sixties indicate that there were, in fact, standards for assignments, some people must have disregarded these standards, as Fields remembers that one professor required two 1,500-word essays from students who could not produce an acceptable 500-word essay. This lack of consistency bothered Fields so much that he requested that a position be created for a director of Freshman English. Hence, in 1968, David Fields became the first director.[27]

Fields recalls that the process of trying to teach composition with the Great Books was "schizo": "You had to spend too much time on the literature."[28] He was hardly alone in his sense of being split between wanting to teach composition and having to teach literature and how to read literature. Bob Cooper, who became department chair in 1970, claims that the demands of even the abbreviated mandated syllabus prevented time for desperately needed instruction in composition.[29] Similarly, Laura Cormack was especially troubled by the fact that most of her instruction in composition took place in individual conferences. According to her, this method was not only an inefficient use of faculty time, but it also meant that many students, often the neediest, never actually received meaningful instruction in writing as weaker students are the least likely to show up for one-on-one work, and of those who do make appointments, less than 50 percent show.[30]

By the late sixties, the majority of the English Department faculty thought that Introductory English should focus on the development of composition skills. This attitude appears to be a function of an acknowledgement that while U.S.U. students often had reading comprehension difficulties, faculty felt most responsible for student deficiencies in writing.[31] Such a perspective was in direct conflict with the educational philosophy behind the Humanities curriculum as envisioned by Millet and Sheehan. In 1965, the founding fathers had not intended that the English Department would own the responsibility for university-wide writing instruction. Their plans for the curriculum included writing and learning how to write in all courses, not just English 101 and English 102.[32] Here, their attitude mirrors that of Douglas Sheehan's mentor, Norman Foerster, who believed, "it is plainly the responsibility of the department of English to afford training in well-organized communication of facts and ideas, by means of constant criticism of constant writing done in the required course, although, if this training is to produce a regular habit rather than a casual capacity, all the other departments must unite in insisting that the writing done in reports, examinations, and the like possess a decent correctness and clearness."[33]

During interviews, several professors indicated that they were aware that this writing-across-the-curriculum (as it is now called) was supposed to be part of the original "game plan." A few even chuckled and labeled this innovation, "another one of those great ideas that never got off the ground." No one, not even Sheehan and Millet, recalled any efforts made at faculty development in this area during the sixties.

Although most faculty report feeling frustrated by the multiple demands of the Great Books curriculum, there were some who were not troubled by the prospect of teaching classics and composition simultaneously. Joyce Campbell recalled that she and her late husband, Robert, did not agree with those who wanted to abandon the Great Books curriculum in order to concentrate on composition skills building. Perhaps their reluctance to do away with this curriculum was mainly a function of the fact that they had been recruited away from Ohio Weselyan at least in part by the prospect of teaching the Great Books. However, Dr. Campbell did acknowledge that she was shocked by the low level of composition skills exhibited by U.S.U. students. ("They were simply not competent. They couldn't give me something I could correct.")[34]

By the end of her second semester at U.S.U., Joyce Campbell had learned something that she considered quite important. She found that the Great Books curriculum could be successfully taught if one was prepared to start the instruction at a basic level (ungraded free writing, discussion of themes and techniques) designed to create "the middle class skills of easy fluency."[35] After doing what she referred to as "starting three weeks earlier with fluency lessons," she rapidly moved students to more difficult, college-level work.

Campbell came to believe that those faculty who were unwilling or unable to make innovative adjustments in order to teach the Great Books curriculum to this new population were doing the students a major disservice.[36] This observation aside, David Field's experiences with the instruction of Introductory English are more typical of a significant number of those who taught this course during the middle and late sixties. Both his sense of the appropriate curriculum and his instructional methodology were transformed by working with the hard-hat crowd. In this regard, he recalls an Upward Bound course he taught on Saturday mornings in 1968 to high school students who were paid five dollars per day to attend class.

Professor Fields' Saturday morning commitment to a community outreach academic program was not atypical for this faculty during the sixties. Paul Peters, a long-time friend of Fields, taught the same Upward Bound course in 1967. Many other faculty engaged in similar work, such as giving poetry readings in local libraries, participating in teach-ins, conducting basic skills workshops and serving on committees coordinating community services.[37]

Fields claims that his experiences with the Upward Bound high school students caused him to "loosen up and become less academic" in his approach to both instruction and class assignments.[38] In particular, he recalls that this class taught him how to teach poetry to students who had almost no previous experience with this literary form. He claims that the lessons that he learned from this class such as how to be less academic and teach through games and a sense of lighthearted playfulness became a permanent aspect of his instruction of Freshman English, as well as introduction to literature courses. The discovery that he needed to change and develop innovative, student-focused (rather than literature-focused) assignments also contributed to his dissatisfaction with the Great Books curriculum. He, like Bob Cooper and other faculty, thought that the often times rigid and conservative working class students needed to have their imaginations stimulated by the curriculum. For Fields, teaching the Great Books to this population was like putting an intellectual straightjacket on both them and himself. He, and others like him, were developing competing notions of compensatory higher education that included the integration of developmental strategies designed to create a bridge of understanding for students with limited backgrounds in both literature and composition.

Douglas Sheehan and the Campbells disagreed strongly with those who held positions similar to that of David Fields. They believed that the Great Books curriculum could and did contribute to significant intellectual growth for U.S.U. students, and that classes taught around this material could be lively, even fun. Sheehan's attitude was probably mostly a function of his extremely positive experience during the forties "bootlegging" classics into the introductory curriculum for returning veterans, while the Campbells seem to have been strongly motivated by their own deeply felt love of classic literature.

Not surprisingly, faculty interviews indicate that a professor's own attitude toward and experience with the Great Books strongly influenced his/her attitude toward instruction of this material. Dr. Campbell admits that she, like most faculty, had a terrible first semester. However, rather than demand an end to a curriculum with which students so obviously had great difficulty, Campbell requested and received permission to teach another section of English 101 the following semester. She was determined to apply the lessons she had learned from failure to the development of a curriculum that included some of her favorite literature. Thus, this medievalist claimed that she gained many new insights into the literature by forcing herself to, "do right by the curriculum and the students."[39]

Joyce Campbell's second semester of English 101 appears to have been a great success. Jude Adams, a current U.S.U. faculty member, recalled the course positively and clearly after decades. With a bit of a chuckle, he remembered how Campbell let him know "in a very nice way" that he was illiterate.[40] Of that class which consisted mainly of veterans and a few women who were admitted at mid-year, Campbell said: "What evolved without my being polemical or inflicting the Great Books on them was a study of violence and the way people react to it. . . . In other words, there was another bridge now, other than the bridge created by the three weeks of remedial work, between the classic works of literature and their experience."[41]

Campbell was able to teach what she describes as "an electrifying course" by leading students to the realization that being violent is part of being human and that therefore the Great Books are fundamentally about what it means to be human. She was unique in her persistence and ability to use the mandated material in an exciting and challenging manner; however, she has much in common with other faculty in that her first year at U.S.U. changed her forever as a teacher. Says Campbell: "It completely changed me from being a more or less authoritarian person who demanded that you knew how to spell all the words right. I used to walk around my class and say, 'If you can't spell a word, just ask me. I'm like the dictionary.' That was the common attitude, that the teacher knew everything and was there to stuff it into these empty vessels."[42]

When Margaret Schneider came to U.S.U. from Bryn Mawr, she, like most of her colleagues, had never before encountered undergraduates like the hard-hat crowd. Nevertheless, after a few deadly silent classes, Schneider began working out an appropriate instructional approach for this new student population. To describe this process, she told a story of taking one bright, verbal and rather atypical student aside to ask what was wrong with the students. "Jonathan" told her that the class was unresponsive, "because they've never had a teacher who asked questions she didn't know the answers to. It scares them! And they are contemptuous of you when you demonstrate that you're thinking things out as you talk, that you don't already have the answer."[43]

Schneider invited this student to talk up in class and help her generate class discussions. Thus, the students engaged in a dialogue with the text which was "accessible to critical response and review" in written form.[44] In this respect, Schneider was much like Campbell in her use of in-class dialogue as a method of "getting the dialectic going."

Unlike Schneider, who had a reputation as a composition theorist when she arrived at U.S.U., many faculty indicate that not only were they confused about how to teach the Great Books in an introductory course, but they were also confused as to how to teach undergraduates with limited language skills. While it is clear that there was a small group of full-time faculty who lacked either the interest or the ability to grapple with these issues, most faculty appeared to have been unusually motivated, at least for a few years, to effectively teach Introductory English to this population. Acknowledging this fact two decades later, Dr. Sheehan deeply regretted that he never had the time to implement a faculty development program similar to the one he experienced at the University of Iowa in the thirties.[45]

In part this lack of formal faculty development was compensated for by frequent, intense department meetings in which a wide variety of instructional approaches were discussed, documented, and dissected. Records of department meetings during this period convey a rich sharing of responses to the literature and assignments. (One memo equating a love of Dante with low intelligence is still comical today.) However, these informal meetings and memos, supportive and lively as they were, did not appear to provide faculty with specific information about the learning styles of new populations or appropriate instructional strategies for students who needed remediation. Instructors remained unsure about how to teach classics to students who had never read "whole books" before coming to the university. Faculty who had experience teaching working class Protestant fundamentalists noted that even a background in Bible readings put those students ahead of the mostly Catholic U.S.U. students who lacked experience with ancient themes and stories.[46]

Recollections and records indicate that during the sixties the talk about students and courses was almost endless because most faculty truly believed that they were in the midst of something very exciting and important. They had as David Fields said, "nothing but future" and as Bob Cooper pointed out, as opposed to the situation in the 1980s and 1990s, there was the sense that any mistake could be corrected; "there was always the hope that something new could fix things up."[47] As academics at the beginning of their careers, the majority of the faculty did, like the university, have "have nothing but the future." This atmosphere was intoxicating for many members of the hard-hat crowd, as well as well as the young professors. Some documents go so far as to suggest an almost magical belief that students could be pressed into learning through the sheer force of an instructor's energy and personality.

Records of assignments and classroom activities reveal the good, the bad, and the just plain silly. One young professor asked her students to make collages of Dante's inferno; while another professor asked students to write personal papers describing "My Walden" and "My Odyssey." Some of the assignments were amazing flops; students became alternatingly bored, irritated, and confused. Other professors were able to guide students through the rigors of the texts but their assignments had little relevance to the literature. And of course, there were those few classes and assignments which caused students to establish their own lifelong relationship with classic works.

Today, reading through copies of many assignments, it is difficult not to be amazed by the difficulty of the language and concepts found in the assignment questions themselves. One wonders how many freshmen were baffled by the directive: "Be vivid, violent, vindictive, and vituperative—Dante was."[48]

The assignments were not only demanding, the grading was hard. Many students who attended class regularly and completed all the assignments still failed English 101 and English 102. Yet, in spite of the failure, the spirit of the Great Books curriculum must have left its mark on the surviving members of the first class who dedicated the 1969 yearbook to "the mighty hard hat: the epic hero"; their language revealing both a lingering memory of the chancellor's opening address to "the hard-hat crowd" and familiarity with classic literature.

The low grades are now a matter of record as is the fact that less than 20 percent of the first class actually made it to graduation, even after Dean Millet lowered the cumulative average necessary for graduation to 1.8 from 2.0.[49]

However, during interviews conducted during the late 1980s, most faculty did not recollect giving lower grades than they did twenty years later, nor did they recall that anyone else gave unusually low grades. The few faculty who still had old gradebooks were genuinely shocked and surprised when their own records revealed to them that they taught classes in which the highest grade was a solitary B. Few faculty had any recollections about the source of such high standards. However, speaking anonymously in the late 1980s, one professor did recall a meeting in the mid-sixties in which Sheehan advised faculty to keep grades in line with standards set at other schools. As this professor recalled, "the chairman made it clear that he thought our grades in English were too high."

A random survey of late 1960s grades reveals the following grade distribution in one section of English 101: 0 As, 4 Bs, 17 Cs, 4 Ds and 3 Fs.[50] According to Tom Cefalo, Director of Admissions from 1965–76, the grade distribution in Introductory English was high compared to the grades given in other introductory courses. For instance, out of 68 students who completed Introductory Physics during one semester in the mid-sixties, 48 failed.[51]

Faculty recollections of life in U.S.U. classrooms during the sixties are only a little sharper than their memories of grading procedures. During interviews, professors tended to remember what they were like so long ago; their idealism, their field of scholarly interest, their politics, even their clothes, better than they recall what went on between them and their students. Of course, they recall dialogues between themselves and unique students who sometimes seem to blur and blend into a memory which somehow becomes transformed into a typical classroom experience. Luckily, one can read a few previously published descriptions of life in the U.S.U. classrooms of the sixties for an accurate portrayal of at least some professors' experiences. A respected journalist who taught the Great Books curriculum for a few semesters during the 1960s wrote of his return to class after a few days of business surrounding the publication of a new book. His fears that the students might have decided to boycott his course after this disruption to the class momentum were completely alleviated when, "several of them came up to the desk, bearing (1) a cake which was decorated with the inscription "Congratulations, Mr. Wakefield" (I am certain I was as moved, if not as deserving, as Mr. Chips or Miss Dove), (2) a supply of Pepsi-Cola, (3) paper cups and plastic forks, and (4) a fifth of Early Times bourbon."[52]

My own experience as a member of the hard-hat crowd includes recollections very similar to the one that Wakefield describes. One cold, sunny winter day, I walked into English 102 and saw that a cupcake with candle sat in front of one particularly large, gruff male student. His face melted into a teary-eyed smile when the professor led the class in a lively chorus of "Happy Birthday."

As a teenage freshman, I did not know then how rare this experience was at an urban commuter college; I only knew that I felt that members of the English Department liked us and cared for us as people who were more than our grammatical errors.

Cupcakes and congratulations aside, by the late sixties, many faculty began to weary of the demands of teaching Introductory English. Some retreated to upper level courses composed of only English majors or became absorbed in administrative work. Recalling their exhaustion with the rigors of introductory courses, several faculty interviewees spoke with admiration and envy regarding the innovative team-teaching approach to Introductory English developed by Ann Roberts and Mark Franklin during this period.

Roberts recalled that she and Franklin began team teaching because it was not only fun, it was a better way to teach. She claimed that teaching alone means that one "loses half the show."[53] According to Roberts, team teaching permits one person to talk while the other pays extra attention to student reactions.

Many faculty mentioned that paper grading was particularly demanding and time-consuming aspect of teaching Introductory English. While team-teaching, Roberts and Franklin devised a system in which they each read all of the papers, but divided the correcting tasks into two parts which they alternated in performing. Because they shared grading, these two professors had the time and intellectual energy to give each student extensive, typed comments on their papers, rather than grades. They believed that this process indicated to the students that they took their work very seriously, and therefore most students started to put more time and energy into their compositions.[54]

These two professors devised their innovation mainly to address many of the behaviors that they saw students exhibiting in their classrooms. With two instructors, it was more difficult for students to simply parrot the teacher without bothering to think. As Roberts told me, "the student in order to say anything on a paper or exam must at the very least choose which teacher to parrot."[55] Many students witnessed a spirited dialogue between two educated literary people for the first time in their lives; this encouraged further dialogue or "multilogue." Hence, students learned how to argue intelligently and forcefully in class and in compositions. Twenty years later, this sort of classroom environment would be considered a "discourse community."

During a 1987 interview, Roberts, who received her PhD from Stanford in the late 1960s, acknowledged that she had always loved the Great Books and that she loved them even more after paying the close attention to the texts which team-teaching demanded. However, even during the sixties, Roberts "seduced" students into reading the classics with a contemporary novel such as Vonnegut's *Cat's Cradle* as the first assignment. Her goal in teaching was to translate the meaning of literature, starting with the student's understanding of a topic to the literature and then back to the student's raised level of understanding.[56] She adds that at no time in this process did she regard her students as limited persons. She and Franklin maintained that they always viewed their students as "adults who had rich and complex lives." Like the Campbells, they saw their mission as showing these undergraduates that the themes present in great literature (man's fate or the necessity of making choices) were present in their lives also.

Joyce Campbell, Ann Roberts, Mark Franklin, and Margaret Schneider found a way to successfully combine reading and writing instruction using the Great Books. All four of these instructors used classic literature as a basis for creating a student-generated dialectic. Although they were able to find a way to make the mandated syllabus their own, this was, at best, only partially the case for the majority of people in the department. By 1969, there was a growing and strong sentiment that it was impossible to teach literature (even with an abbreviated syllabus) and composition simultaneously in English 101.

A November 19, 1969 memo from the Freshman Committee indicates that most faculty felt that 101 should no longer be an introduction to Western literature. Rather, the memo stated "that a primary task of a department of English is to develop its students' skills in writing and speaking English."[57] The committee proposed that the study of literature be delayed entirely until English 102, and that only English 111 and 112 function as introductions to world literature.

Those faculty who considered reading and writing instruction to be two separate phenomena believed strongly that these subjects required separate methods of instruction and should therefore be taught in separate courses. Of course, this attitude flew in the face of Millet and Sheehan's educational philosophy and it also troubled some members of the English Department, notably Margaret Schneider. In a memo dated December 8, 1969, Schneider blasted those who believed that reading and writing should be taught in isolation. "In freshman English, everything has to happen all at once or it's likely that it won't happen at all," she wrote.[58] Schneider appeared very frustrated with faculty who believed that the low skill level of the student body was a reason to alter or water-down the curriculum. Quoting George Steiner, she declared that we are all "language animals" and therefore rhetoric should allow students and faculty to, "develop that common condition into a resource for learning."[59]

Schneider believed that literature should be used to stimulate the questions that students wrote about ("Everything the writer sets down is an answer to a question.").[60] Like Joyce Campbell, she found the notion that great literature was too demanding for the hard-hat crowd a disturbing proposition. However, unlike both Campbells, Schneider did not advocate a continuation of the Great Books curriculum which she considered, "a genteel notion left over from the days when the idea of a gentleman's library was popular."[61] Instead, she advocated that students give serious attention to a collection of carefully selected paragraphs written by major thinkers, such as Kierkegaard, John Donne, or D. H. Lawrence. Her intention was that these selections would focus on a specific theme or issue which would become the basis for dialogue, analysis, and dialectic.

Because she was interested in combining the instruction of reading and writing without the Great Books, Margaret Schneider might have been able to formulate a viable departmental alternative to the either/or approach to instruction that viewed either writing or reading as primary, rather than integrated. It appears that this never happened because Schneider, although she had a national reputation as a composition theorist, held little power within her own department during this period. (To what degree this is because she was a part-time faculty member is unclear.) In fact, during 1969 to 1985, she sent out roughly 12 memos initiating faculty development or composition-focused projects which not one colleague responded to in writing.[62]

Schneider does not know why no one responded to her efforts to create a forum for discussion of the instruction of reading, thinking, and writing. (Her theoretical perspectives do, however, play a role in the formation of the composition theories of those who led the Freshman English program in the 1980s, 1990s, and into the 21st century.) History also does not tell us why her memos met with a wall of silence, which their author interprets as disinterest. What we do know is that by the end of the sixties, Dr. Sheehan was a relatively powerless faculty member who had been replaced by Chester Hunt as department chairman and Robert Campbell as head of the Humanities Division. The Great Books curriculum was on its deathbed as faculty nibbled away at the syllabus in order to find time to focus on the writing deficiencies of the hard-hat crowd. In this regard, one could say that as a department, the English faculty were moving away from a "sink or swim" approach to freshmen instruction centered around classic literature, and toward instruction in freshmen writing designed to teach composition skills neglected in weak urban public and parochial secondary schools.[63]

·4·

A HOUSE DIVIDED, 1970–1971

Tin soldiers and Nixon's comin', we're finally on our own.
This summer I hear the drummin', four dead in Ohio.
NEIL YOUNG (FROM "OHIO")

Whatever their opinion of the Great Books curriculum, the vast majority of the English faculty were student-focused regarding this subject, rather than concerned with public policy or institutional issues. Hence, their dissatisfaction with student response to the curriculum led many professors to push for a major transformation of the curriculum of Introductory English. As Bob Cooper pointed out, this was no easy task as Sheehan had presented the department with a well-organized fait accompli in 1965. Individual attempts at reform were fragmented and therefore it was difficult to compete with the status quo. It took years for the divided and frustrated department to gain any sort of consensus about a new curriculum. Therefore, Sheehan's curriculum comprised the basic form of Introductory English throughout the sixties.

Change was inevitable. The downtown campus itself was a metaphor for an institution in conflict. During 1965–70, classes were taught to the tune of sledge hammers and constant construction as offices and classrooms were created or remodeled. Most English classes took place in an old red brick structure with large, dirt-coated windows and dreary, dusty rooms that offered students a less than inviting first impression. By the late sixties, classes were frequently terminated early by bomb threats. After many months of almost daily empty threats, the braver faculty and students remained in classrooms to voluntarily continue instruction.

The noise and clamor seemed part of the times—a time of war in Vietnam, sporadic warfare in the cities and rapid and sometimes radical social change.

The noise was often an annoyance, but at other times it appeared to some to be the birthing moans of a new kind of college and even a new society.

Faculty descriptions of this period of "creative chaos" at the new public university in no way parallel Allen Bloom's portrayal of the sixties as a time when university professors exhibited, "servility, vanity and lack of conviction" as they fawned over radical students who were "nothing better than a rabble."[1] Perhaps Bloom's made-for-TV depiction of the sixties is an accurate reflection of several months at Cornell in 1969. However, his picture of faculty-student dynamics is not an accurate portrayal of even one day during this period at U.S.U. where the young, or at least youthfully energetic, faculty were mostly to the left of the commuter students who still held many of the same values as their lower-middle and working class parents. There was some student activism, but it was for the most part low-key and pragmatic. The most publicized student demonstration was a 1970 sit-in for day-care led by student mothers and their pre-schoolers. As I recall, the hard-hat crowd was struggling to find time for study, work and families and considered protracted protests a luxury they could not afford.

Yet, the war in Vietnam was always part of the atmosphere of those early years. Veterans returned and entered classes. Tables with leaflets detailing anti-war activities or analyzing the military-industrial complex were in the halls as well as in the many times condemned (by the Board of Health), grimy student cafeteria which was located in the basement of the building in which most English classes were held. In fact, many students and faculty cited the war as a major reason to abandon the Great Books curriculum. They wanted to spend their precious hours for study reading and writing about this contemporary and crucial topic, rather than Homer's *Odyssey*.

Gerard Daley, working in the university's president's office during the late 1980s, spoke matter-of-factly about the curriculum changes which occurred during this period.[2] Unlike Stephen Millet, who continued to remain loyal to ideals expressed in the 1945 "Redbook," Daley was basically unaffected by considerations of the status of the Liberal Arts within public higher education. As a politician rather than an academic, Daley believed that the new university's curriculum simply evolved to fit its constituency. Somewhat similarly, then chancellor, Dr. Albert Galvin, believed that the school's founding fathers were "carried away" when they tried to create a working class Harvard, instead of moving in a direction "more appropriate" for local working people.[3]

Clearly, Galvin was referring to Millet in particular when he spoke of the founding fathers who had overly ambitious, if not elitist, ideas about the place of the Liberal Arts at an urban state university. At a 1987 presentation at an Ivy League Graduate School of Education, Galvin presented himself as a man of the people as he talked about building a university where busy first generation college students acquired a sound education. Yet, Dean Millet was equally passionate when he reflected on the academic needs of working class students. As a child of a local blue collar family and a scholar of French public education, Millet believed he understood the critical needs of first generation college students who should be, he argued, in the process of moving beyond a provincial mindset, and acquiring an education for thinking citizenship. In a 1979 letter to a local alternative newspaper, the first Dean reaffirmed this position, dramatically asserting that he did not believe that the republic was likely to survive unless most people received a classic education.[4] Here, his attitude mirrors that of English Professor Margaret Schneider who, in 1969, took an equally passionate position when she stated in a memo to the Department: "English teachers have a moral and political responsibility to make literature at least available to their students. Otherwise, a literate and sophisticated Third World will one day confront an illiterate, visually aided West."[5]

In contrast to Millet and Schneider's philosophical perspective, Galvin and Daley kept their eyes on the promise of a middle class lifestyle that a college degree could provide. A hallmark of their leadership was access to middle class professions. Such an individualized or private mission for a public university represented a critical alteration to the original mission which emphasized, in stressing the importance of an educated citizenry, the needs of democracy over the individual.

In contrast to the state, national or even global perspectives of politicians and philosophers, most English faculty seemed to view their classrooms as mini-societies. They often tried to create a sense of a small community. As educators motivated to create personal and social change, they saw "the English Department as an instrument for confronting, if not correcting, past errors."[6] To correct the past errors of rote learning and dreary lectures that stifled the imagination, faculty felt they needed new curricula.

These were heady days. It was not unusual to walk into a faculty office and see a banner proclaiming, "Revolution in Our Time." The revolution was waged with words. Many faculty wanted the content of their courses to empower students, to enable them to analyze and understand their culture and country. Other instructors appeared more interested in creating a course that would guide students to greater self-awareness. The faculty goal of getting students thinking and dialoging was really not much different from Millet's goals. The difference was in the content of curricula.

Within and outside the English Department, there was a general dissatisfaction with the mandated set of Core Course requirements that had been in operation since the school's beginning. To many faculty and students, these courses represented not only an elite tradition of liberal arts education; they also symbolized an oppressive culture that was dismantling a non-western culture in Southeast Asia.

As the war dragged on, students and faculty became increasingly intolerant of the demands of the traditional curriculum, which seemed not only to transmit the values of a destructive society, but also deprive them of both time and intellectual energy to study contemporary and compelling topics and issues. This situation reached a point of no return in the spring of 1970 when the United States bombed Cambodia illegally. Almost immediately, student protests against the invasion occurred at U.S.U., as well as most college campuses across the nation.

In the spring of that year, students were shot and killed at Jackson State University and Kent State University while demonstrating against the bombing of Cambodia. Many people who were students during that period recall feeling that their society had attacked them, that the guns of war were now turned on them. At the urban commuter campus, posters sprang up proclaiming, "America eats its young!" I saw the same angry words at every campus I went to that year. College was no longer fun and games. Kent State and Jackson State proved that campus politics could be serious stuff. For a while, the "felt beanie crowd" ceased to exist on most campuses; many students felt that they too wore a hard hat. Nationally, a significant number of students and faculty voted to strike from classes. Instead, students attended teach-ins and meetings about the war.

Elizabeth Curtis, a faculty organizer during the strike, recalled that this was the only time in the school's history that large numbers of students and faculty spent a great deal of time together on extracurricular activities.[7] Freed from classes and course requirements, many students received their first taste of collegiate bull sessions. I, along with others, attended city-wide meetings held at nearby elite colleges, entering buildings that had intimidated most of us since childhood and mixing for the first, and often only, time with students who had attended prestigious private high schools.

It was an era when many old distinctions mattered little. Both faculty and students recall that the boundaries between these groups became thin to nonexistent. For young faculty, this often felt like liberation from the traditional rigidities of academe. Many students also felt exhilarated by the openness between students and faculty; but others recall feeling disoriented and confused by the sudden lack of structure and authority. Both students and faculty remember that, for a while, the subjects involved in their coursework seemed insignificant and trivial when compared to the struggle to end the war and the dynamic community that they created together.

Many faculty and students recollect that it was difficult to get back to business as usual in the fall of 1970. The strike had changed relationships between students, faculty, and curriculum. To many, formerly acceptable standards and grading criteria seemed punitive. Speaking decades later, Dr. Curtis recalled that she was no longer the same kind of teacher she had been in 1968.[8]

Elizabeth Curtis was certainly not the only professor whose attitude toward pedagogy and curriculum was changed forever by the student strike. Notes from the University senate (representing all faculty and students) indicate that by 1970 there was a good deal of organized opposition to the core requirements which many faculty viewed as authoritarian impositions on students. Faculty and students expressed a range of opinions concerning the negative effects of the requirements during this period. It seems that there was a great deal of deeply felt concern over the fact that over 65 percent of the students in the first two classes had dropped or flunked out of school because they could not succeed in the introductory courses.[9] Such considerations had even motivated Dean Millet to lower the cumulative average necessary to graduate in the class of '69 from 2.0 to 1.8.

Records of meetings of the University Senate indicate that almost all faculty and administrators were worried about low student performance. However, there was heated disagreement about how the curriculum could respond more effectively to the student population. Some felt that the wisest thing to do was to join the ranks of the many schools that had abolished all or most of their required courses. Others felt that while it might be O.K. to scrap course requirements at more affluent private schools, the hard-hat crowd needed to take required coursework that compensated for their weak secondary school education, as well as their deprived home lives.[10] One professor reasoned that since the average U.S.U. freshman had lower SAT scores than students at local, competitive private colleges, a rigorous set of requirements seemed appropriate in order to bring these students up to the standards set by students at higher performing schools.[11]

The message behind statements like that above is clear and, according to the then director of admissions, it was also indicative of a position held by many faculty who seemed to him to want to teach a more homogeneous student population than U.S.U. offered.[12] These instructors believed that if working class students performed academically like middle class students, they would be better off. According to former Admissions Director Tom Cefalo, professors who had this attitude taught their introductory courses to the level of the most capable students and let the others fall by the wayside. With bitterness in his voice, he noted that they appeared to be completely unconcerned about the low retention rate.

The majority of the membership of the University senate no longer wanted to "spoon feed" students required courses and curricula designed by the founding fathers. The cry for relevancy and self-directed studies was heard throughout meetings.

About the same time the required courses were being debated in the senate, the English Department was receiving and reviewing many proposals for a revised Introductory English curriculum. The bulk of these proposals were written between 1970 and 1971 and submitted for consideration to the Freshman English Committee. Two things are most striking about these proposals: the amount of literature to be assigned and the political orientation of the majority of texts selected. Although faculty had argued vehemently that Introductory English should focus on composition, the bulk of the proposed syllabi were literature heavy. Most curricula were designed to provoke inquiry into the nature of western, capitalistic society or the self in society. Commonly assigned texts were Achebe's *Things Fall Apart*, Kesey's *One Flew Over the Cuckoo's Nest*, Vonnegut's *Cats Cradle*, Fanon's *Wretched of the Earth*, Huxley's *Brave New World*, de Beauvoir's *Second Sex*, and *The Autobiography of Malcolm X*.

It is interesting to note that although faculty frequently said that the Great Books were too demanding for underprepared and overscheduled undergraduates, their most commonly selected texts do not actually reflect a lowered reading level or slimmer volumes than the classics. What is different is that the subject matter of the literature and the themes of the courses proposed are more congenial with faculty interests in contemporary issues.

Elizabeth Curtis's plan for the revision of Freshman English is the forerunner of the proposal that was eventually accepted by the University Senate on April 10, 1970. Earlier that year, Curtis had written a proposal which did not add her "list of favorite Freshman English techniques and texts to the growing collection of lists now circulating."[13] Instead, she recommended that "a number of English 101 courses be offered, that the titles of these courses be listed in each semester's schedule of courses, and that descriptions of the various courses and reading lists be submitted to enrolling students along with the schedule."[14]

In her proposal, Curtis cautions faculty against making their courses too literary, saying, "The 'literary' approach to freshman writing is ideal for English instructors and English majors; it is less than ideal for the student who has never been confronted with 'good literature' before and never hopes to be again."

The revision of Freshman English reflected much of the philosophy expressed in Curtis's proposal and ignored most of the perspectives held by faculty such as Schneider, the Campbells, and Doug Sheehan, who felt that the department had an obligation to introduce students to literature. The spirit of the new proposal affirmed two main points, that the end goal of 101 and 102 should be the effective practice of writing, and that instructors should be allowed to choose means, "congenial to their own imaginative purposes" to accomplish this goal.[15]

By the academic year 1970–71, the revision had passed the senate and English 101 and English 102 became "a year's practice in writing," rather than the first two semesters of the Great Books curriculum. Many faculty report that they began using anthologies and thematic readers at this time, mainly because they weren't quite sure what else to use and because they wanted to assign readings that everyone in the class would have time to finish.[16]

During 1970–71, although hotly contested, the core requirements remained in effect and all students had to take English 111 and English 112 or a literature in translation course. Most students chose to enroll in English 112.

All through that transitional academic year, although English 101 and 102 no longer introduced students to the earlier classics, English 111 and 112 remained an introduction to 19th- and 20th-century literature. Several faculty report that both students and instructors generally enjoyed these courses and invested a great deal of intellectual energy in them. It was not uncommon for students to sign up for the same professor for both semesters. Hence, classes usually had an intimate atmosphere, sometimes including birthday cupcakes and other personal gestures of care and concern. After the requirements were abolished, English 111 and 112 remained very popular courses, even among students who did not major in English.[17] Because these courses focused on modern literature, faculty frequently experimented with new curricula and instructional approaches in these sections. One professor taught a course which focused on women and literature, while another taught an introduction to the experiences of Black people in the nineteenth century as well as an introduction to non-western literature. Still another young professor taught literature that explored man's attitudes toward his natural environment. Although the courses mentioned above were popular and the faculty energetic and skillful teachers, it is probably important to note that none of these faculty members received tenure. Hence, their role in the creation of introductory curricula is limited to this historical period.

In the development and presentation of most of curricula for English 101–112, "relevancy" became the magic word. Literature and assignments were frequently viewed as tools to aid the development of a political perspective and an enhanced self-awareness. Students were often asked to identify and analyze cultural stereotypes and images (Example: "We will examine age-old Western images of womanhood and the particular 19th century manifestations found in the literature."[18]). Here, the instructor's goal was more than finding something to write about; she/he was bringing students into the heated debates that were taking place across the nation, particularly on college campuses. Although both students and faculty seemed to believe that their rejection of the traditional and embrace of the relevant was a new idea, in fact, the emphasis on writing about contemporary rather than classical subjects and texts echoed ideas about writing instruction during the Progressive Era of the 1920s, another time of economic boom and rapid social change.[19]

The spirit of the times affected most of the members of the University Senate. On March 25, 1971, this administrative body voted to abolish the original course requirements established by the founding fathers. During the debate preceding the vote, these men were once more accused of trying to turn U.S.U. into a working class Harvard. However, the mood of the times was a bigger factor in determining the vote than whether or not the original curriculum was elitist. The fact was, as Dr. Bruce Hamilton, the then chairman of the University Senate, was quick to point out, the disenchantment with required courses was part of a larger trend on college campuses across the country.[20] At that time, the majority of college faculty would probably have agreed with one Professor of Physics when he said regarding the notion of requirements, "I am against compulsion."[21]

Levine points out that this period of curriculum reform "was a by-product of the 1964 Free Speech Movement at the University of California at Berkley." He states, "the causes of campus unrest were frequently non-curricular, but the resulting soul searching brought to light student dissatisfaction with the post-Sputnik mentality and curriculum that emphasized the needs of society but failed to consider the needs of the individual student."[22]

The above perspective is expressed in the notes of the University Senate by a student who likens the U.S.U. curriculum to his "six years of prison" at a competitive public examination school. Interestingly, the student's hostility to the classical curriculum prompts several faculty members to express concern over his attitude. One such professor quickly responds to the student by telling him that he is lucky to have had a coveted slot in such a fine public school.[23]

In a way, the above impassioned exchange between student and faculty epitomizes the nature of the dispute over curriculum at U.S.U. Educators who stood by the virtues of a curriculum such as the one offered at the selective public exam school believed in the benefits to be gained by pulling one's self up by this school's intellectual bootstraps. However, as Bruce Hamilton explains, the university had to acknowledge that the traditional philosophies of higher education which were appropriate in the 1950s did not apply to undergraduates at this public urban university in 1971. Although the reasoning behind his point of view was unclear, Hamilton made this point as confidently as the savvy politician, Daley, made his.[24]

As one leafs through the University Senate notes, one gets the impression that although rarely mentioned, *The Working Paper for Education at Brown University* influenced the vote that finally eliminated the core requirements. This more than 400-page document written by two Brown University students, Ira Magaziner and Eliot Maxwell, strongly expresses the view that education should be an experience that is self-directed, rather than dictated by extensive requirements.[25] In the language of the day, Magaziner and Maxwell essentially advocate that students should be able to "do their own thing" academically.

Working Papers was a provocative and timely document which was most likely read, or at least discussed, by many faculty involved in university governance. The spirit of the recommendations of the undergraduate authors can be found in the Senate proposal for curriculum reform, which was accepted by the university community in 1971:

A. A pattern of courses as follows. With the exception of (1), they may be taken at any time during a student's undergraduate career, but students are advised to complete them as early as possible.
   1. One year of training in writing to be taken in the freshman year.
   2. Courses in foreign language as follows: Students who demonstrate proficiency in a foreign language at the intermediate level shall be exempt from a language requirement. Students who meet the entrance requirements regarding language or who otherwise demonstrate elementary proficiency in a foreign language shall take one year of a foreign language at the intermediate level or one year of a foreign literature in translation. Students who do not meet entrance requirements in a foreign language will be expected to satisfy them by taking one year of elementary language work at the University, and then to take the year at the intermediate level or the year of literature in translation.
   3. Three terms of course work in the social sciences, of which at least one must be taken in History and one in another discipline.
   4. Three terms of course work in the natural sciences or in mathematics, of which at least two terms must be taken in the same discipline, and at least one in a natural science.

B. As an alternative to (A) a student may choose to design his her own core curriculum, in consultation with a faculty advisor or with an advising committee. Guidelines for the operation of this advising procedure are to be worked out by a committee of the Senate, and implementation of the self-designed core curriculum must be preceded by Senate approval of these guidelines.[26]

Option B, the program for self-directed studies, was consistent with the reforms advocated in *The Working Papers* as well as the mood of the times which emphasized the individual's right to choose everything from whether or not to fight in a war to which courses to take. Although many students and faculty were initially excited by this alternative, less than five percent of U.S.U. students actually pursued this curriculum option during the early seventies.[27] In reality, the university never had the resources to facilitate this sort of academic program on a large scale. Likewise, the local public and parochial schools which most undergraduates attended rarely prepared students for independent thinking, let alone self-directed study.

Even at Brown, the student-focused Modes of Thought program did not catch on as its authors had envisioned. The voluntary nature of the program, coupled with the complete abolition of general education requirements, led most students toward early specialization, rather than self-directed exploration of Liberal Arts subjects.[28] A similar trend toward a more career-focused orientation was even more likely at a public commuter college where the vast majority of students were strongly motivated to gain a credential that might become their passport to a middle class lifestyle.

For U.S.U. students and faculty, the end of the 1970–71 academic year meant the end of the much-debated Core Course requirements, as well as the Great Books curriculum. A new era was beginning in the life of this six-year-old institution. As part of this change, the required curriculum of Introductory English was now two semesters long, rather than four. As a function of the 1970 transformation of English 101 and 102, these courses were now described in the university catalog as, "a year's practice in writing." Hence, it was now required that all undergraduates receive training in writing, but not necessarily exposure to any complete literary works.

·5·

THE RECONSTRUCTION PERIOD OR THE RELEVANCY-BASED CURRICULUM, 1971–1974

Together we look for an institution that makes neither Alexandria nor Bologna nor Woodstock nor Hue alien to us. The ideal is never reached, but even the process of partial failure enriches the ideal.

CHANCELLOR FREDERICK M. COOPER
1971

The above quotation does not contain an uplifting message; it is not expressed in language we are accustomed to hearing from university leaders. Cooper's rhetoric is far removed from the ennobling words of Chancellor Dooley who confidently declared in 1965 that the new university would be a place where dedicated hard-hat scholars would become knowledgeable in all the liberal arts. What caused this change to occur only six years after the university opened its doors? Many people say that they simply got realistic; Stephen Millet says they became less innocent and consequently less hopeful.[1] He also remembers that the second chancellor, fresh from a major curriculum revision at his last institution, believed that the original curriculum was "hopelessly out of date." In the mid-1980s, Chancellor Albert Galvin maintained that by the early 1970s the university was in the middle of a process of developing a curriculum that was more responsive to the students it served.[2] One wonders why such a transformation was dubbed a "partial failure"; such words seem to indicate the abandonment of an ideal, a dream deferred.

The academic year 1971–72 began during a time of "partial failure." The nation was losing the war in Vietnam, as well as the trust and respect of many of its citizens. Under President Nixon, the federal government was beginning a retreat from the battlefields of the War on Poverty. The brief era of New Frontier liberalism which had given birth to the new school had come and gone. It often seemed, after the assassinations of King and the Kennedys, that only ghosts had dreams.

The early 1970s also marked the beginning of negative media depictions of college. In the spring of 1972, CBS ran a special entitled, "Higher Education: Who Needs It?" Strongly biased against the value of a four-year degree, the program closed with the startling statistic that of 1,200 students registered at a state university placement office, only sixteen received job offers.[3] Given the lower cost in time and money and their vocational emphasis, similar stories predicted accurately that the decade would see a rise in attendance at community colleges. Such practical concerns, coupled with negative reactions to media depictions of violent student demonstrations, led many to question the value of a baccalaureate degree.

Yet, there were those among the founding fathers who held fast to their former vision of public education, refusing to give Woodstock equal billing with Alexandria. They rejected an education that focused primarily on relevance and utility, continuing to believe in the timeless value of an education that not only benefited the individual, but also served the public good. Dr. Alan Paine, who later became a dean at a nearby private college, recalled that during his 1970 interview for a position in the English Department, Dr. Millet was particularly impressed with this candidate's undergraduate major in the Classics. Behaving as if it were still 1965, the dean vigorously impressed Paine with the importance of teaching traditional content to undereducated college students, and probed for agreement with his educational philosophy.[4]

Although Paine recollected that Millet emphasized traditional course content as part of the mission of this urban liberal arts college, it is interesting to note that most long-time faculty remember that the school's original mission was to provide a first rate education to local public school graduates. Most long-time faculty do not recollect that this mission was tied to a particular curriculum. This belief may be part of the explanation for the fact that most faculty and administrators with whom I have spoken claim that the school's original mission has remained unchanged since 1965; yet analysis of curricula changes and statements made by key university officers reveals that by 1971 undergraduate education had changed profoundly.

The president of the flagship campus, Dr. George Stone, had been working since his inauguration in 1970 to steer the urban campus away from an identity as an elite-style liberal arts institution, and toward an identity as an institution geared toward education for "utility." This utilitarian perspective caused him to have a low regard for the educational priorities of the founding fathers. In December of 1970, Stone put himself on the side of practical and political men such as Senate President Daley when he was quoted in the press as saying: ". . . new models must be found for university education in the state. Our liberal arts education derives from the days of Cardinal Newman and the idea of training for a leisure class. The language requirement—recently under siege on the urban campus—can be seen as a remnant of the conviction that no gentleman should be ignorant of Latin and Greek. Similarly, our sometime preoccupation with graduate students and graduate schools comes from a venerable tradition of scholarly elitism that is now in sharp collision with the harsh facts of supply and demand."

During the early 1970s, the city's largest newspaper described Stone as "a man of imagination and much resolution, one who understands power and knows how to use it." Certainly, his allegations that faculty at the urban campus were delivering miseducation in the form of "scholarly leisure studies" to hard working residents had to be a powerful influence for curricula change. Likewise, his political sophistication allowed the President to operate successfully within the constraints imposed on his administration by both the private sector which viewed U.S.U. as a competitor for Liberal Arts students, as well as the state legislature which was reluctant to fund higher education that was not in step with the realities of the contemporary job market.

While some members of the English Department, such as former department chair Phil Soule, spoke positively of Stone's "practical" effect on curriculum, others viewed him as an enemy of the Humanities. Bob Cooper, who became chair of the English Department in 1970, spoke of Stone as "against us." In the late 1980s, he claimed that Stone "wanted to keep us something that was according to his definition, urban." As Cooper sees it, Stone's policies translated into "no stepping on the toes of the flagship campus" with duplication of programming and replication of the type of traditional university which the ideology of the 1960s and 1970s labeled a failure. For U.S.U., this would mean no graduate programs and a market-driven notion of the scope of liberal arts. According to Cooper, a major problem with the imposition of this "utilitarian" philosophy was that most of the full-time faculty had been recruited to the university for their success with and knowledge of traditional curricula. They were, in fact, part of the scholarly elite. They, like the Harvard-educated Cooper, may not have been all that wild about the mandatory Great Books curriculum, but they were even less enthusiastic about teaching in an institution that might never have graduate students and emphasized college-level survival skills, especially when Millet had, "all but promised" them extensive graduate and research programs during the late 1960s.[5]

Cooper's observations are representative of more than his personal disagreement with state-level policymakers; his perspective also reflects a sharp contrast between the interests of state government in higher education and those of many faculty. During the mid-1970s, this state continued to have one of the lowest per public higher education student expenditures of all the fifty states.[6] Therefore, Stone and other university administrators were staying in step with state-level policies and priorities when they advocated a basic and practical orientation to public higher education. Although Cooper spent several years as a university administrator, he remained an academic at heart; as such, his natural sympathies were not with the interests of state government or even the state economy. His identity was always tied to his conceptualization of what any good university should be doing for its students. According to his philosophy, the quality of an education should be measured by standards that are mostly unaffected by economics and politics.

In the early 1970s, while President Stone was talking about "utility" and Chancellor Dooley was coming to terms with "partial failure," the faculty of the English Department were trying to reconstruct course curricula, both introductory and upper-level. Regarding this process, several faculty mention that their attitude toward Freshman English remained similar to that expressed in a statement issued by the Freshman English Sub-Committee in 1970 when it was decided that Freshman English ought to become a year of writing instruction. That statement was developed in order to clarify the new nature of the first year of English after the demise of the Great Books curriculum. This document affirmed that the primary aim of Introductory English should be, "to impart to freshmen the habits of thought and the linguistic skills presupposed both by our advanced courses and by university education generally." This translated into the rather vaguely expressed notion that English 101 and 102 ought to prepare the student to use, "if not elegantly, the resources of the English language both to clarify his thinking and to communicate in writing."[7] Regarding literature, the document states that, "although readings are integral to the design of the course, they must subserve its basic aims; the instructor must conscientiously endeavor to make certain that the number of texts (as well as their length) and their content do not allow the course to turn into something other than a course devoted primarily to writing."[8] Within this context, faculty were to teach the skills of defining, analyzing, comparing, distinguishing, describing, discerning and testing premises, drawing conclusions, and marshalling and assaying evidence.

Given that it took years of discussion and feuding to piece together the 1970 alternative to the Great Books syllabus for English 101 and 102, it is not surprising that the next few years were characterized by hostile disagreement among faculty about everything from grading standards to text selection to attendance policies to teaching styles. As Ohmann notes in *English in America*, this period was one that was characterized by reform of Freshman English curricula across the nation, with an emphasis on "freedom and relevance."[9] As

Zack Joplin reminisced in 2003, the beginning of this decade was a time of anarchy, confusion, and chaos.[10] One gets the impression that this unstructured period was very different from the "creative chaos" described by David Fields[11] only a few years earlier.

The disagreements were so unpleasant that some professors felt compelled to issue memos that pleaded for an end to the bitter, exhausting, and often fruitless arguments. Still others questioned the very existence of the introductory composition-focused course. Voicing "more concern about the gifts and limitations of the students who don't drop out than those who do," Wilfred Skye took the extreme position that, "Perhaps it is unnatural for most people to be skilled as writers. Perhaps it is wrong to make them so."[12] As Bob Cooper pointed out, unlike the 1980s when a well-selected committee could make decisions with little opposition, everything had to be discussed during this period.[13]

David Fields, who was still Director of Freshman English during 1971–72, can clearly recall "the amazing pain" of those years. According to him, abandoning the Great Books and dismantling the Core requirements were easy and clear-cut issues when compared to the question of how to teach writing to inner city college students. Although most faculty were pleased and relieved that they could now turn their attention to the development of writing skills, many instructors also had extremely strong feelings about the very act of writing comments on student papers and presenting these same papers in faculty meetings for collective comments. This attitude was particularly common among the fast growing population of part-timers who, according to Cooper, comprised about 20 percent of the English faculty by 1972.

Professor Stephanie Peterson, who was also involved in designing a policy for the inclusion of Afro-American curriculum materials, was furious at the notion of judging any student, particularly inner-city African Americans.[14] She and other faculty members maintained that it was inappropriate to write negative or evaluative comments on student papers, that comments should reflect a nonjudgmental acceptance of whatever level of literacy a student had attained. Somewhat sarcastically, Fields maintained that faculty in this camp saw their proper role as, "cheerleading the students to emotional heights."[15] He believed that many of these instructors viewed themselves as social therapists full of almost infinite understanding who could gently guide students to enhanced expressive capabilities by raising their self-esteem.

Faculty who acted as so-called social therapists often viewed meetings of the freshman writing staff as oppressive impositions. According to Fields, they had principled objections to group discussions of student papers. Because they felt that comments about students' work had to come from a knowledge of and sensitivity to a given person's life and background, they resented the assumption that a group of academics had a right to evaluate the work of an anonymous student.

There were some faculty who considered this nonjudgmental, therapeutic approach to instruction to be too soft and not in the students' best interests. Fields recalls that Father John Riley, who taught in the English Department for two years in the early 1970s, epitomized faculty who refused to believe that a teacher needed to have a personal understanding of a student in order to comment on his work or teach him successfully. Fields recalls that Riley was outraged at his colleagues' attitudes. He believed that effective teaching demanded that faculty have standards that were not individualized. According to him, loose, flexible standards only left weak students stuck in ruts created by poverty, racism, and functional illiteracy.[16]

While the contemporary reader may be tempted to trivialize the nature of these heated, often hostile debates that occurred among the freshman writing staff, it is important to remember that they were very much a part of a larger debate which was occurring nationally on college campuses. Students, particularly minority students, were demanding that faculty examine the origins of their standards and assumptions about curricula, grading, Standard English, and the use of power and authority.[17] Many faculty recall, as does Dr. Fields, that such confrontations were both intimidating and the source of much confusion about the appropriate role of instructors, especially teachers of low-income and minority students.

Part of faculty reluctance to judge and criticize came from a desire not to reinforce or continue oppressive practices and patterns in students' lives. Their refusal to evaluate student work by traditional standards was part of their growing awareness that many of their students had been short-changed and belittled by an educational system that often judged them harshly, unfairly, and superficially with constant and inappropriate references to white, middle class criteria and values.[18] Not wanting to be part of the problem, these instructors were often unsure about the role they should play in the college classroom of the 1970s. They had abandoned the red pen held in a heavy hand; and they were in the process of experimenting with instructional approaches which they believed would lead to learning without failure, and without censor.

On a national level, the confusion was not limited to the question of the professor's use of authority; there were many other perplexing issues confronting educators involved in higher education during this period. In a January 1972 report from the English Department at City College of New York, Chairman Theodore Gross asked, "What happens to a department that suddenly finds itself offering 50 percent writing courses? . . . What happens when older professional staff, untrained for the new remedial work, have fewer electives as part of their program?"[19]

Dr. Gross was concerned about how CCNY could continue its tradition of humanistic training for a new generation of college students when open admissions policies presented faculty with a type of student who needed a level of remediation for which they had little preparation. Essentially, Gross's report asks the wider academic community how they can both continue to offer a college level education and meet the academic needs of this new undergraduate population. He claimed that the issues he confronted were problems that "confront any urban or state university that no longer adheres to a traditional mode of education or that, in one form or another, commits itself to Open Admissions."[20] Certainly, the chairman's concerns were relevant to the English faculty at U.S.U. in the early 1970s where they too were coming to terms with the reality that a growing percentage of their departmental offerings were introductory service-level courses.

In many ways, the friendly "we're-all-in-this-together" atmosphere of the sixties was destroyed by the bitter feuding about how to teach underprepared students. Laura Cormack recalls a department meeting in the early 1970s in which the exact nature of the conflict was summed up well for her by Patrick O'Neil who said that the department was divided between those who believed in passion and those who believed in pattern.[21] O'Neil considered himself to be in the passion camp which included those who believed that a teacher had to know his students well and create a curriculum that had a powerful relevance to their lives and times in order to improve their writing. He said that the believers in pattern were always searching for the right instructional methodology, the perfect model for skill development. These faculty, like Father Riley and Laura Cormack, did not feel obligated to relate personally to their students. Quite naturally, there were those among the faculty who pointedly defied neat categorization into either the passion or pattern camp. In a memo dated April 10, 1972, Dr. Chester Hunt, the second chairman of the department during the late sixties, clarifies the perspective of one professor torn between "freedom vs. control." Addressing this dilemma, Hunt said, "And what that complexity seems to me to require is that, in the conflict between the spokesmen for tradition and the spokesmen for experiment, we come down squarely on both sides at once." Hunt eloquently defended his position in three pages which culminated in the statement that art itself is always full of the tension between passion and pattern: "Though all that the poet, novelist, painter or composer does originates in some free personal response to life, he is forever committing himself to choices which impose their own consequences and limit his freedom."[22]

Of course, it was not the feuding alone which ended the camaraderie that had characterized the early years of the English Department. Urban State University was a much larger place by the early 1970s. By 1972, with a head count of 5,630, the school was almost five times its original size.[23] The combination of increased size and scarce resources meant that many part-timers were hired to teach the introductory sections. These temporary, poorly paid instructors could not possibly make the investment in time, energy, or enthusiasm that the full-timers had. Also, innovations designed to create unity and involvement were often sabotaged by factors beyond the control of the department. For example, an effort made to encourage faculty to join one of four groups that would develop introductory curricula around a similar theme was rendered ineffective by commuter student schedules which were usually a function of timeslots, rather than interests.[24] Thus, faculty could not assume that a given student was motivated to consider "writing and socio-political ideas" just because she had chosen a particular 10 o'clock section of English 102.

Laura Cormack recalled that during the semesters immediately following the abandonment of the Core requirements, most faculty, regardless of whether they believed in passion or pattern, developed syllabi which focused on the theme of the self and self-knowledge. This topic was frequently a given for those who relied on thematic readers, as the majority of the texts of the period, like Gillespie and Stanley's *Someone Like Me*, also focused on self-awareness.

Cormack remembers that the exploration of the self initially established a positive, upbeat classroom climate, as most faculty believed that they were providing the students of the flower child generation with something they wanted and something they needed at this point in their lives. However, during the year, the course content rather quickly shifted to a more society-based orientation when faculty discovered that the self-centered curriculum had the potential for invasion of privacy, and frequently set students up for writing overly self-conscious, tedious essays.[25]

If faculty once believed that the Great Books curriculum was all that prohibited them from teaching composition successfully, they surely must have been frustrated by the level of writing competency exhibited by students during the early 1970s. While several professors recall that the students who attended the university during this period seemed to attain somewhat higher levels of writing proficiency than their predecessors, there were still many students who came to U.S.U. so unprepared that the problems posed by the expectation that they would gain college level writing skills often seemed overwhelming to faculty who struggled to devise curricula which could lead students from grade school skills to mature writing.

In the freshman class of 1972, 35 percent of the students had Verbal SAT scores below 450; this was a big drop from the test scores of the previous year when only 12 percent on the freshman class scored below 450.[26] The above figures may or may not include some Special Admission students as students who entered the university through Special Admissions were not required to take SATs as they were evaluated by nontraditional criteria. By 1971, roughly 12 percent of the freshman class was composed of Special Admissions students who did not fulfill traditional college entrance requirements.[27]

Some of the pressure put on instructors of Introductory English to respond to the needs of underprepared students was, at least theoretically, alleviated by the Special Admissions Summer Program, English 005, which was created to provide students with a pre-freshman summer experience designed to develop high school level competencies in critical reading, writing, and thinking. Students who did well in this course could receive credit for English 101 and continue onto English 102 in the fall. Students who experienced less success in the course did not receive any credit for their summer work and moved into English 101 in the fall. Obviously, this situation put pressure on both students and teachers to get and give credit for English 005.

Of course, many of the mostly adjunct faculty who taught the special summer courses experienced the same ambivalence about judging, correcting, and criticizing their mostly minority, low-income students as did full-time faculty. In fact, these often younger, less experienced instructors were frequently the recipients of pressure for high or lenient grading from politically sophisticated and angry students who resented being singled out for special handling which included the possibility of taking a course for which they would not receive any credit. Needless to say, many of these students moved into English 102 with less than high school level skills.[28]

The heated discussions about large general, political issues seemed to keep faculty from getting down to discussing the nitty-gritty of approaches to teaching composition to students exhibiting a wide range of writing abilities. Hence, faculty were mostly on their own in the development of curriculum. Left to devise their own plans, many faculty, such as Laura Cormack, used much of the time freed up by the absence of lectures about literature for in-class writing activities. The products of these activities could be reviewed by the teacher in class or shared with the whole group. Many instructors refer to this method of writing instruction as much more productive than the approaches they used during the 1960s when, according to Cormack, composition could only be taught in individual conferences or in the form of comments on papers. This methodology was not only a very ineffective use of faculty time, it also left out many students who either didn't make conference appointments or didn't attend to paper comments.

Marie DeGaule, an adjunct faculty member during the early 1970s, recently compared the undergraduates in her sections of Freshman English to those she taught at a nearby private college. Like most part-timers, she had missed the tumult of the early years, and was flush with both enthusiasm and confusion similar to that experienced by the original full-timers. For her, teaching at U.S.U. was much more difficult than teaching at the competitive, private college. But, she said recently, "It was an exciting time because it felt as though this school was conducting an experiment about educating people who didn't at all fit the mold of the usual college student. But it was very hard work, and it felt to me at that period in my career to offer a great deal of frustration regarding the training in and measurement of real improvement in the skills I wanted to teach: skills in critical reading and interpretation, and the writing of clear and, I hoped, expressive prose." Although the hard-hat crowd did occasionally surprise her with "bursts of eccentric and original expression," DeGaule found teaching at the private college "a totally different situation." In that setting, "the students who came to my section were self-selected to reflect my and their interest in contemporary poetry. These undergraduates did the reading; not extensive, but intensive, and they came to class willing, even eager to participate."[29]

Alan Paine, who became the second director of Freshman English in the fall of 1972, recalled that his own confusion about what or how to teach English 101 and English 102 was a function of the fact that he had never taught or taken an Education course prior to being hired in the fall of 1970. He was not concerned about, nor does he recall thinking about, a teacher's larger role in society. He just wanted to survive 1970–71. Resorting to the only instructional model available, he ended up teaching a course designed from his recollections of Introductory English at Amherst College which he attended as an undergraduate during the early sixties.[30]

Dr. Paine recalls that during his first two years at U.S.U. he enjoyed talking to his colleagues about what they were doing in Introductory English. He also remembers that he even enjoyed talking to salespeople from educational publishing companies in an effort to learn about the latest and best selling texts in composition instruction. These conversations provided him with many references which were useful to him as he struggled to design a curriculum which was more than a hazy carbon copy of his own undergraduate instruction. As director of Freshman English for College I, Paine worked very hard to expand this dialogue about what works with Freshman English to all those engaged in teaching these courses.[31] Although the new urban campus was a hot bed of disagreement and discussion about almost every topic, one issue the second director never had to deal with was whether or not the instruction of introductory composition should be under the control of the English Department. This was not the case at all urban campuses on the East coast; in 1972, at the University of Maryland, College Park, the faculty senate attacked the freshman writing program for "serving the interests of the English department rather than the interests of the university."[32] Things could have been even more complicated than they were.

In 1972, the College of Arts and Sciences was divided into two colleges. College II had a more traditional curriculum, which included fixed course requirements in foreign language, science, math, and Western Civilization. This division into colleges had almost no effect on the curriculum of Introductory English, as there was little difference between the two English Departments. However, there were two department chairs, William Evans and Bob Cooper, and faculty had to select college membership.

Although nobody seems actually to recall the rationale by which the colleges were divided, according to one silly campus legend the department was divided according to one's opinion of an eccentric older faculty member who claimed to have been intimate with many famous writers, as well as to have participated in the Spanish Civil War.[33] Supposedly, College II contained all those faculty who either tolerated or sat at the feet of this charismatic woman who taught many of her classes from the bedroom of her nearby apartment, rather than come to the university. However, her influence on the curriculum of Introductory English would have to be described as all but non-existent as she rarely taught freshman writing, never held an administrative position, and all but exclusively interacted with students who majored in English. Although completely unfounded, the persistence of this campus myth indicates the existence of a lingering spirit of light-hearted camaraderie.

Department data indicates that one of the few differences between the departments was that all freshmen in College I were required to complete a one-hour writing sample during orientation. This was probably a function of Cooper's long standing belief in accountability and consistency. At least two faculty evaluated these essays, and advised the weakest students to enroll in a remedial section of freshman writing, English 110. Sections of English 110 were smaller than the typical section of English 101; fifteen students at the most enrolled in these remedial courses which included access to at least one hour of individual conference time per week.[34]

Alan Paine claimed that he was chosen to be the College I director of Freshman Writing because he was willing to take on a job that most older, more experienced faculty found too time-consuming and tedious. He recalled that the majority of his time was spent "counting heads," rather than curriculum or faculty development projects. He remembered hours and hours spent leading students from room to room, dealing with checklists and other routine paperwork.[35]

However much Paine saw himself as a department functionary in the position of director of Freshman English, data indicates that he was also committed to at least the idea of faculty development, if not the implementation of specific programming. Departmental memos from 1972 and 1973 are full of references to talks and presentations which Paine and his partner in College II, Liz Vermeer, organized for the benefit of those who were trying to develop effective approaches to the instruction of composition. Although these presentations were well publicized and often given by nationally known experts, they were usually poorly attended.[36] Although a few faculty mention that some of this programming influenced their curriculum (a presentation by Robert Lyons, director of Freshman English at Queens College, is occasionally cited), by the late 1980s most interviewees could no longer remember that these presentations ever took place. One can only speculate that by 1972, faculty were so exhausted by the 1970–72 arguments over large, general issues that they had lost the inclination to attend meetings about curriculum. A 1972 memorandum from the chairmen of both departments underscores the problem of attendance at staff meetings. In it, Evans and Cooper almost beg instructors of Freshmen English to treat scheduled meetings as "serious obligations."[37]

As Paine recalled, he focused staff meeting time mainly on the issues of grading and papers comments during his first year as director. As both these activities involved the potential for judging, criticizing, and evaluating students, they were of interest to most faculty. In the spring of 1973, in response to significant faculty concern over the issue of grading, Paine proposed to the College I English Department that the traditional grading system be replaced by a grading system that would allow faculty the flexibility to grade A, B, Pass, No Credit. This system was designed to allow those students who were motivated by high grades to receive grades, while at the same time permitting those who were inhibited by grades to avoid them.[38] Obviously, this proposal was strongly motivated by the prevailing educational philosophy that encouraged instructors to grade students on the basis of individual growth, rather than a single standard of competence. However, Paine's grading system never went into effect, and fifteen years later he was amazed at his own ignorance of the many policy implications which were inherent within that then seemingly simple recommendation.[39]

During 1973–74, Paine and Vermeer focused staff meetings on curriculum development. Paine recalled thinking that even though faculty viewed themselves mainly as a group of radicals, they were resorting to some very conservative approaches to teaching Freshman English. In an effort to stimulate new ideas about instruction, he invited faculty to give presentations focusing on a successful class they had taught or a successful sequence of classes. Faculty shared the basic assumptions behind their courses, as well as how they ran their classrooms. Paine remembered that, as innovative as some faculty were, they (himself included) related to the courses as if the professor controlled the whole show. In retrospect, he came to believe that this attitude forced students into the position of having to give the right answer, rather than think and write from their own evolving perspective.[40] Certainly, students in teacher-centered classes could not be partners in the learning process.

Paine's observation about instructional methodology during this period is a very interesting one. There is little evidence to disprove his theory that faculty thought they were responsible for almost everything that went on in a course. Although most faculty were very concerned about social equality, the notion of collaborative learning which could have functioned as a potent model of equality in the classroom community was not yet current.[41] Most discussion and assignment questions were designed to lead students to an awareness of either their role in relationship to other people or the role of sexism, racism, or imperialism in their lives. These questions appear to have one right answer that the teacher already knew and the student was supposed to find. This instructional methodology gives the teacher control of the class, but it does not lead the students to new questions and uncharted waters. The teacher waits for the students to "get it," while the students may resent being asked questions for which the teacher already has the answer. Frequently, students responded to this form of guessing game with nonresponse, leaving faculty wondering why students refused to get involved.

Only a few professors, such as Margaret Schneider and Wilfred Skye, asked questions for which they didn't already have an answer. Even the courses that were structured around a politically leftist theme featured assignments which were designed to bring students to one correct analysis. Today we may find it strange that faculty who were very concerned about criticizing and evaluating their students were not particularly interested in becoming partners with their students in the teaching and learning process. It seems they were concerned about their potential for abusing their authority as teachers, but they did not think to question the basic nature of that authority. In the classrooms of the early 1970s, freedom meant liberation from traditional texts and punitive grading standards; but faculty remained in control of the reading list, assignments, and most interpretations of assignments. Students were lead to the water, there to drink the instructor's truth.

As part of his personal effort to break away from the teacher-centered approach which he had observed in most introductory courses, Paine co-taught a section of English 101 in the fall of 1972 with Wilfred Skye who was the biggest influence on his development of pedagogy.[42] This course did not have any required texts other than a blank notebook, which was placed in the school bookstore as the assigned text. The purpose of the uniformly assigned notebook was the creation of a class identity which the two professors hoped would lead to a class spirit.

True to their desire to make students partners in the learning process, Paine and Skye developed a course intended to, "give our students some systematic method for generating discourse."[43] It was their sense that syllabi and rhetoric texts too often focused on the form and structure of finished papers and neglected to give students a method for generating their own compositions.

The course was structured around conversations overheard by students. During the semester, students collected and recorded conversations, later expanding these conversations into a piece of expository writing that placed the conversation in a context by describing who was talking and where. During the middle and later portion of the semester, students recorded a conversation with a selected individual, and from that data developed a portrait of the person with whom they conversed. The last course assignments focused on analyzing these portraits and the nature of the conversations, and turning a conversation into an argument for a certain point of view, i.e. a heated political debate might serve as a portrait of one of the debaters and an argument to vote for a certain candidate.[44] It is interesting to note how much this innovation is a sort of foreshadowing of the "discourse communities" created in Freshman English classes in the 1990s and discussed in Chapter 9.

Paine viewed his student-centered curriculum as very successful. It allowed him to avoid many of the pitfalls of the relevancy-based curriculum, such as assigning literature about drugs or the generation gap to mature adult students who could not take these topics seriously, or waiting for students to come to the right answer about a contemporary issue. The "conversation curriculum" allowed students more control over their work and allowed Paine to teach composition as he felt it should be taught. It was his belief that a composition course ought to (1) develop a sense that there is a difference between an experience and the language used to describe an experience, (2) give training in the formation of ideas and concepts about a particular subject, (3) teach students how to construct arguments, and (4) teach students how to locate a writer or speaker's argument, indicating main ideas and supporting details.[45]

In 1974, Paine taught the conversation course alone. The second time around, he added some assigned reading; this time requiring students to read personality profiles written by Norman Mailer, Truman Capote, Tom Wolfe, and Joan Didion. These authors were read in connection with the profile writing assignments. Thus, students could see that the focus of a portrait was a matter of personal choice; Mailer quickly leaves his subject to engage the reader in a Byzantine meditation on the American Hero, while Capote sticks with Brando, letting his subject's own actions and words tell his story. This addition to the curriculum permitted students to understand the range of possibilities available to them as writers, again creating an awareness that there is no one right way to write about a given subject.

Although Paine claims to have had little knowledge of adult learning or literacy theory at the time he developed the conversations course, one can't help but wonder if he, at least, was not greatly influenced by the outside speakers he invited to those poorly attended meetings of the freshman writing staff. Many of those speakers, such as Robert Lyons, explored the unique literacy needs of adult learners in a public university. Certainly, this director's understanding that the relevancy-based curriculum held little interest for many older undergraduates, indicated an awareness of the learning styles of many mature students whom Cross indicated often prefer learning experiences that provide both structure and opportunities for self-direction.[46]

During the two years that he was director of Freshman English, Paine engaged in other collaborative teaching projects. He did this out of the belief that there ought to be more in common to the introductory course than practice in writing. Paine was not alone in his belief that distinct curricula for almost every section of Freshman English was not the best way to run a program. However, it appears that the fact that most faculty took part in the 1969–71 curriculum revision process led to the desire to teach a course of their own design. Hence, most instructors were reticent to move toward any collective conceptualizations of the Freshman English curriculum. They were enthusiastic supporters of the academic freedom implicit in the system that had been in effect since 1970.

After a year's experience as director, Paine became more convinced that faculty needed texts and/or assignments in common in order to have productive conversations about instruction.[47] According to the director's mentor, Wilfred Skye, without common texts and assignments, meetings would always deteriorate into debates about larger issues. After all, everyone was talking about a different course. For example, Patrick O'Neil's students read the daily newspaper, while Joy Swanson's students were still reading and writing about the literature of the Great Books. Skye reasoned that a shared syllabus would create a bigger and more focused investment in meetings of the freshman writing staff; thus, instructors might talk about how best to teach the curriculum, rather than the more general issue of how to teach or grade.[48]

Paine became involved in another collaborative project when he joined a group with Matthew Gormley, Wilfred Skye, and Laura Cormack. Drawn to the contemporary theory that it was better to teach one text thoroughly than several texts too quickly, they all agreed to teach a section of English 101 using one required book, *The Education of Henry Adams*.[49] The four met frequently, creating common assignments, and reviewing the text and student responses. Speaking years later, both Paine and Cormack acknowledged that although this activity was intellectually stimulating for the four academics, their courses were not all that successful. Paine believed that they did not pay enough attention to the readability of the selected text, a book which held great interest for them, but was too demanding and "old-fashion" for the students.[50]

In the fall of 1974, Alan Paine left the position of director for two years of research in Poland. Speaking fourteen years later, he maintained that he was not a particularly important player as far as the story of the curriculum of Freshman English is concerned, in spite of the position he held for two years. He believed that the big influences on the curriculum were faculty such as Schneider and Skye who could never be bothered to take on the management tasks required of the director, but who nonetheless were major thinkers and scholars in the area of college writing instruction. When asked how these two influenced the department when most of their attempts at initiating faculty development were all but completely ignored, Paine replied that he did not know. However, he still believed that these two brilliant, idiosyncratic, and innovative teachers and theorists did influence the curriculum, at least the spirit of the curriculum.[51]

·6·

RELEVANCY RECONSIDERED OR THE HONEYMOON IS OVER, 1974–1977

I think we could all improve the writing of our students if we moved somewhat closer to the systematic coverage of basic tools and skills that is a feature of 110.

BOB COOPER
1975

Bob Cooper became the director of Freshman English during a period when "our students were simply not well prepared."[1] While some faculty cite the sixties as a time when Urban State students were often extremely underprepared for college work, Cooper claims it was the middle seventies, when the university moved to its permanent location that brought him into classrooms full of students who were both weak academically and generally unenthusiastic about academic subjects or studies. In contrast to the eager but underprepared students of a few years earlier, many in the classes of 1978–1982 acted as if they had little reason to attend college. Brint and Karabel note that this period coincided with media coverage that portrayed college as losing value in terms of lifetime earnings; several headline articles described overqualified college grads flipping burgers or collecting unemployment compensation.[2] Further undermining enthusiasm for higher education was the belief current among the general public that the country was in the midst of a literacy crisis. With the publication of the often-referenced article, "Why Johnny Can't Write," which declared that the nation was "spawning a generation of semiliterates,"[3] there was a good deal of cynicism and suspicion surrounding the practice of teaching reading and writing at any level.

In reality, during the first two years of the life of this new university and briefly during the middle seventies, this institution had all but open admissions. In 1965, U.S.U. had to accept as many students as possible in order to justify its existence, while in the mid-1970s, at the beginning of a state fiscal crisis that was further eroding state support for public higher education,[4] Chancellor Silvio Mitrano felt pressure to fill the newly constructed Oceanside Campus. Situated near the then infamous Abraham Lincoln Housing Project, the campus location seemed to be frightening away potential suburban and/or middle class applicants. Therefore, in 1974, when applications for admission were down by 3,000, the admissions office had to find a way to increase its enrollment figures.[5]

It does appear, according to numerous faculty interviews, that while the skill levels of the underprepared students of the mid-1960s and 1970s were somewhat similar as measured by SAT scores, the students who came to the university in the mid-1970s were much less motivated to "do college" than their predecessors. Or maybe, *Newsweek* was right, and this new crop of students suffered from a lower level of basic literacy than those who attended college in the previous decade. Or, perhaps, they were influenced by the atmosphere of "partial failure," or maybe somehow student morale was affected by the years of struggle which students and faculty (led by former Dean Millet) waged against the move from the heart of the city to the unpopular Oceanside Campus site. Interestingly, in a 2002 interview, Millet mentioned that by the early 1970s, he had personally developed a plan that would have allowed the urban campus to remain in the downtown location, close to the city's libraries, theaters, and museums. The school's new location on a perpetually clogged expressway was sarcastically dubbed "the commuter campus no one can commute to."

But, it is also possible that student malaise had nothing to do with the unpopular relocation or gaps in literacy skills or even the poor job market for college graduates; it may have been the case that students at U.S.U. were only part of a larger national anti-academic trend created by the early specialization that was characteristic of this period. This emphasis on early specialization, coupled by shortages in professional jobs, created an institutional climate that was both suspicious of intellectualism and disinterested in civic involvement and political activism. In a column in a September 1973 issue of the student newspaper, the editors blasted their fellow undergraduates for ignoring their responsibilities as members of a college community. One student journalist lamented that, "never in the recorded history of this university has student apathy reached such a low. One student from College I attended the discussion last week on the adoption of a permanent College I constitution."[6] The student voices in this editorial bitterly regret the lack of interest displayed by current students who were the recipients of college governance rights won by students who entered the university during the 1960s. Their anger at their peers causes them to ask; "If the students of College I pretend that they can decide to abrogate their responsibility for the actions of their college, which touch each individual in it on a day to day basis, then we wonder what other more remote responsibilities they will ignore. Vietnam? Chile? ITT?"[7] This short piece of student writing captures the divide that was developing between the students who identified with 1960's style activism and those students who were more interested in education for a specialized credential. One also has to speculate about possible connections between the type of general education that the editors of the student newspaper would have received before 1971 and the almost requirement-free curriculum experienced by the more apathetic students of the mid-1970s. The ideas inherent in the language of the student editors regarding the obligations of citizenship in a democracy are implicit in the required readings of the original core curriculum, but knowledge of these concepts was not generally an aspect of the curriculum experienced by the students who failed to attend college governance meetings.

When Bob Cooper became the director of the freshman writing program in 1974, the English Department had been living with four years of almost complete faculty freedom regarding the development of curricula for Introductory English. He appears to have considered this essentially experimental, free-form program to have been something of a chaotic mess in which faculty felt it didn't even matter whether students took English 102 first, or the other way around.[8] This state of affairs prompted Cooper to strive to provide the writing program with order, sequence, and consistency.

Unlike Paine, who saw his job mainly as a lower-level managerial position, Cooper expected to have a major influence on practice by guiding the department to a collective definition of both English 101 and English 102, and providing a consistent sense of logical and gradual skill building.[9] As a tenured professor, former department chair, and former director of the freshman program at two elite private colleges, Cooper was in a much better position to exert strong leadership than the young and inexperienced Alan Paine. In fact, as the man who had been most responsible for the abolition of the mandatory Great Books curriculum for Freshman English in 1970, Cooper was in an optimum position to engineer curriculum change.

Cooper's work as director was also made somewhat easier, or at least clarified, by a 1974 job description authored by Phil Soule in response to Paine's understandings of this position.[10] It appears that, at that time, Soule was the heir apparent to the position; however, previous commitments to other courses kept him from assuming the position until 1976. Cooper made his acceptance of the directorship contingent upon departmental acceptance of Soule's description of the position of director of Freshman English for 1974–75. Essentially, this document grants the director the authority to actually direct, rather than simply manage, the program. This job description gave Cooper the power to both oversee course design and text selection and begin the process of setting some uniform standards for the introductory courses.

Cooper's tenure as director marks the beginning of a period in which the Director played the starring role in the story of the introductory curriculum. By 1974, the full-timers had reduced their commitment to Freshman English and subsequently the role of part-timers had increased. Hence, Cooper and those directors who followed him tended to exert more forceful leadership in matters of curriculum and pedagogy than their predecessors. This situation was mostly a product of two factors, the status of most part-timers and the concern for university-wide policy issues, such as writing proficiency.

During his two years as director, Cooper began the lengthy process of devising a list of commonly held standards which both defined what students needed to know in order to function competently in Freshman English and specific pedagogical objectives for teachers. As outlined by the director in a 1975 memo to the writing staff, the proposed pedagogical objectives read as Figure 2.

The generation of the list that came to be known as "the minimal abilities" accomplished two things; it set a process in motion which led to the development of a remedial Freshman English (English 010) for students who did not have minimum abilities for freshmen, and it established the first criteria for what was to develop into a college-wide examination of writing proficiency.

As a self-described type A personality, Cooper was extremely frustrated by the lengthy debates surrounding both the contents of the list of minimum abilities and the very notion of proficiency testing. It seemed that for every standard he proposed, there were several people who were willing to argue for many hours against its use as an instructional guideline or a necessary competency.[11]

In 1975, as part of his efforts to assure that all undergraduates achieved a bottom line of writing competency, Cooper forwarded a request for approval of a new course, English 010, to the College I Senate and the Department of Academic Affairs. This proposal gave him, as director of Freshman English, more control over curriculum by granting him the final decision as to who would be advised to enroll in 010 and who could be exempted from one or both semesters of the freshman writing requirement. These decisions were to be a function of an evaluation of a writing sample read and reviewed by at least two members of the department.

FIGURE 2 Proposed Pedagogical Objectives

Semester I	Semester II
Sentence Agreement Consistent tenses Three primary sentence patterns beyond simplest predication ("The cat is on the mat," "This book contains many interesting characters.") a) lists b) balanced phrases and clauses c) causal relationships	Parallel construction Subordination Appropriate diction A repertory of more than one logical scheme or pattern Meaningful sequencing
Paragraph Unity and Coherence: clear thinking as represented in a logical scheme of some sort.	The time for learning how to make grammatical and rhetorical choices for emphasis and clarity, & for developing a facility in more sophisticated techniques of revision with more complex composition problems. A legitimate aim is a paper that takes account of two views of a topic.
Composition emphasis on pre-writing, the discussion and demonstration of how to generate a topic, to frame a definition, to develop a thesis statement and to support with examples. An awareness of revision. The capacity to compose a paragraph paper is a legitimate aim.	As much can be learned in working the short paragraphs from outside sources as from a large body of research materials, but various kinds of term papers may be required. To write in a variety of sentence patterns To be correct in spelling, the use of quotation marks and capitals, the use of articles, the use of "and."
Syntax, Grammar and Mechanics: To establish useful relationships between clause and clause. To correct the number and tense endings of verbs, the use of possessives, the main uses of the comma and the semicolon, the use of pronoun form and reference, the use of multiple negatives.	To establish clear relationships paragraph, sentence to sentence. To frame a definition, develop a thesis statement and to support with examples. To deal with outside material from at least two sources.

FIGURE 2 *continued*

Composition: Logic and Rhetoric To unify paragraphs. To develop a contrast and comparison. To make the paper as a whole coherent.	To establish a voice appropriate to the subject matter, the occasion and the audience To avoid wordiness, jargon, and the excessive use of the passive voice.
Style: Voice, Diction To display these abilities with reasonable consistency in a five paragraph paper.	To display these abilities with reasonable consistency in a paper of more than six typewritten pages.[12]

Cooper's proposal for a new remedial English course meant the termination of the existing remedial course, English 110. This course had served as an intensive English 101, consisting of smaller classes and extra private conferences. After completing 110, students moved directly into English 102. Under Cooper's new plan, most remedial students would move from English 010 to English 101, rather than 102, thus allowing English 010 to function exclusively as a pre-freshman experience. Cooper felt strongly that academically weak students needed this extra time and practice to develop their mastery over more difficult kinds of writing assignments. Regarding this policy decision, he wrote, "Although the success of EN110 is gratifying, the English Department has come to the conclusion that the combination of En110 and either 102 or another writing-credit course does not adequately serve the needs of a number of students."[13]

Most faculty were reluctant to teach English 010. Both the instruction of basic grammar and composition skills and occasional work with learning disabled students were unfamiliar territory to academics who had been trained in traditional doctoral programs. To help chart the course in unknown waters, Cooper developed a sample thirteen-week syllabus, detailing weekly assignments and review topics, as well as a required reading list that included *Webster's Dictionary*, a handbook of current English, and the *Harbrace English Workbook 7B*. To offer further support for both students and faculty, a plan for utilizing student tutors was also created.

In developing his plan for peer support in English 010, Cooper drew upon an existing resource in the form of an upper level English course in advanced composition and tutorial. This course, which had been providing majors and student teaching candidates with the opportunity to assist in U.S.U. classrooms since 1973, was enhanced under Cooper's leadership to include specific programming for the use of tutor time and orientation and training for tutors. Under his plan, upperclassmen received review in basic skills, which they often needed in order to support remedial students confidently. In a further effort to put more teeth in this tutoring experience, students were also required to write an academic paper about their work.

Cooper was the first director of Freshman English who was interested in exerting a significant degree of systematic control over curriculum. In 1975, as part of his effort to understand what students were learning in all sections of freshman writing, he conducted a statistical analysis of the relationship between patterns of grading in freshman sections and performance on a commonly and voluntarily administered writing sample. He discovered that there was little relationship between students' grades and their ability to write well as evidenced by their performance on the writing sample. Cooper's major finding was that there was too much difference between the skill levels of the students enrolled in sections of English as a Second Language 102 and the rest of the students taking English 102. He also found that the range of abilities exhibited in all sections of English 102 was generally extremely wide.[14]

Cooper was troubled by the findings of his study because he believed that an extremely broad ability span was destructive to the potential of a class. Hence, he wanted to create more uniformity in both the outcomes of English 102 and the freshman writing program in general. His discovery that some faculty were "amazingly successful" at teaching almost all students the writing skills necessary for competent performance on the writing sample, while other courses produced A students without writing proficiency, convinced him that there ought to be an exit examination of writing proficiency for all sections of English 102.[15]

The students in Laura Cormack's sections of Freshman Writing scored the highest on the writing sample, even though they did not have the highest course grades. Cooper shared this information with the department in a memo, which also contained his general findings. More specific information regarding the correlation between scores on the test and course grades was shared with faculty privately. It is interesting to note that at the time of the test, Cormack was one of the few instructors who viewed English 101 and English 102 not just as English courses per se but as preparation for all undergraduate writing.[16] Because of this orientation, her syllabus was interdisciplinary in nature (containing no more than one literary work) and she focused on a range of specific skill building, the selection of which was a function of what she perceived the students most needed in any given semester, as indicated by writing samples. For example, if students were having difficulty distinguishing complete sentences from sentence fragments, Cormack did not burden them with instruction in the use of the apostrophe.[17]

After sharing the results of his test with the department, Cooper tried to generate support for an exit exam from English 102.[18] He believed that this instrument would have many benefits for the university, the department, and the students. From his perspective, the exam would have at least three positive outcomes: pressure instructors to teach the skills tested, guarantee that students acquire minimum competency, and respond to the need to train students to write proficiently in all courses taught in the College of Arts and Sciences.[19] However, the majority of the members of the English Department did not respond to Cooper's plan positively. In fact, this proposal resulted in another period of long, bitter departmental debates, which eventually concluded with the defeat of Cooper's plan for an exit exam.[20]

The arguments against the test ranged from the assertion that the exam would be unfair to minority and foreign students, to the notion that it was putting too much weight on one particular occasion. Many faculty believed that the exam itself was only a test of a student's ability to write in a manner that was artificial, dull, and unimportant. Basically, the majority of the members of the English Department felt that a solid, reliable evaluation of a student's writing could only be done by someone who had worked with the student over a long period of time.[21]

Cooper recalled that during the lengthy and sometimes bitter debates over the exit exam, he had some extremely angry things to say to some colleagues, which he later regretted. But, such was his commitment to and belief in the necessity of consistent standards for Freshman English. At that time, he told faculty that if the English Department didn't come up with its own test of writing proficiency, the College would, and the department would lose control of the process. (Of course, what he did not realize was that no one department would ever want sole responsibility for guaranteeing the writing competency of the College's undergraduates.)

While most faculty were aware that there was campus-wide dissatisfaction with student writing skills, they were still against the imposition of an exit exam. In fact, many faculty subscribed to a theory created by the findings of an informal study conducted by one faculty member who discovered that students' writing abilities actually declined when they became upperclassmen.[22] This idea reinforced English faculty thinking that other departments were responsible for the low level of writing proficiency, and that their grades should be the only evaluation made of student writing proficiency.

Cooper was not convinced by the vocal majority in the English Department. He stuck by his belief that if the department was going to have an 010 and a 101 and a 102, it ought also to have clearly articulated minimum standards for entrance and exit for each course. If this was not done, Cooper believed that the department would be failing its students. This belief became central to Cooper's work at the university. During 1979–80, in the position of Associate

Dean, he worked to implement a new Core Curriculum college-wide. A major commitment to minimum competency in writing was central to the design of this innovation.[23]

Bob Cooper's student-focused, competency-based perspective is fairly unique in the world of higher education. He is a scholar, a researcher, but also, a teacher. Unlike most members of his department, Cooper took Education courses while working on his doctorate in English at Harvard. Out of his experience in a Theories of Education course taught by Israel Schleffler, he decided to explore and apply for public school teaching positions, a choice rarely made by Ivy League PhDs.[24] Although these explorations convinced him that he did not want to work with the high school age group, there has always been something of the dedicated public school teacher in this academic whose scholarship focused on questions about curriculum, learning, and teaching.

Phil Soule, who followed Cooper as director of Freshman English in the fall of 1976, had a similarly long history of involvement with introductory curricula. During the late 1950s, he was assistant director of Freshman Composition at a large midwestern state university where he experimented with innovative instructional methods long before they became known as "the new grammar" or "sentence combining." Basically a loner in his practice, Soule simply developed techniques that seemed to work with a given group of students; but he did not view himself as someone who studied composition systematically. He, like many other U.S.U. faculty during that period, was surprised when his little classroom activities turned out to be hot selling educational theories when conceived of and marketed by someone else years after he had been saying things like, "Here are 3 sentences, put 'em together."[25]

During the early 1970s, Soule was in charge of the graduate program at a prestigious public university where his involvement with the college was all but exclusively devoted to graduate level instruction in English. Under pressure from the Dean, he had admitted almost all of the 150 students in the graduate program, "even though, we knew by that time that the jobs for these people had all but dried up." Feeling "more and more dishonest," Soule began a job search for a position in an institution dedicated to undergraduate teaching. The English Department at Urban State was almost as far away from a "top heavy prima donna" atmosphere as he could get.[26]

A self-described long time Marxist, Soule said of the student population that greeted him in 1972, "I knew that I wanted these people as I had heard about them." However, his longing to work with the hard-hat crowd was quickly replaced by a sense of frustration and confusion. When reflecting upon this period in his life, the late Dr. Soule was refreshingly honest and sharp: "I realized I didn't understand this diversity and how to deal with it. Then it was frustration because I was totally unprepared for the fact that people would come for two weeks and then disappear." His ideological commitment to the hard-hat crowd did little to prepare him for the daily realities of working with students who "seemed to hardly be able to stay alive," let alone attend a university.

Soule gave careful thought and consideration to the issue of teaching introductory courses to working class commuter college students. He seemed to have a handle on one of the "problems that has no name" in the literature of higher education: "I had been told that they worked two-thirds of the time or full-time outside. So, I knew that. But, it hadn't occurred to me that that was going to force a complete rethinking of my rhythms and plans for a course." Like most academics, Soule was a great planner, and his sense of course sequence was based on the attendance patterns of traditional age students at middle class residential colleges; for him, "it was very difficult to plan out a course when people were so in and out."

Not only was Soule perplexed by the issue of erratic attendance, but he found himself also challenged by the practical, utilitarian orientation to learning held by the hard-hat crowd during the early seventies. Even though he claims to have been comfortable with the utilitarian priorities of President Stone, Soule was briefly knocked off balance by students who demanded a more authoritarian teaching style from him. Unlike his former students who wanted freedom to explore their own ideas and theories, Soule observed that for many urban students the work ethic, "informs the value of almost all activities." These students demanded that he give them something that could be transformed into a marketable skill. Freewheeling or exploratory assignments were frustrating to students who seemed to be saying: "I pay you to teach me. Teach me."

Some of Soule's insights into the hard-hat crowd were facilitated by his earlier teaching experiences; by 1956 he realized that "the most competent writers often had nothing in their heads." Probably this revelation created the kind of awareness that lead Soule to believe that some undergraduates who had not yet acquired writing proficiency were, in fact, "the brightest and most interesting students I had ever taught." For, although many of these students were not competent writers, according to Soule, his classes had the "highest intellectual level" of any he had ever taught. Regarding this statement, it is important to note that many U.S.U. faculty, including some of those most thoughtful about Introductory English, never mentioned experiencing this high intellectual level which Soule and others, such as Joyce Campbell and Ann Roberts, spoke of as part of the reward of teaching the hard-hat crowd. Interestingly, almost two decades later, interviewee transfer student Jake Stein spoke of the dissonance between the high level of class discussions and the level of analysis required to perform well on written assignments and examinations.[27] He was perplexed by the simplicity of assignments that followed complicated discussions; but one can speculate that Stein's professors were responding to the same academic limitations that Soule noticed in his intelligent students years ago.

It was undoubtedly Soule's commitment to the intellectual energy and curiosity of the undergraduates that caused him, as chairman of the English Department in 1972–73, to institute a policy requiring all full-time faculty to teach Freshman English three out of four semesters. Over time, this policy evolved to allow for scheduling pressures placed on the full-timers, as well as lobbying by faculty who taught other kinds of writing courses and wanted to be exempted from freshman instruction.[28] However, a glance at the Fall 2002 registration bulletin indicates that even the semblance of Soule's requirement was not in effect 30 years later.

When Phil Soule became director of Freshman English in 1976, he had just finished three years of developing, implementing, and teaching the first Law and Justice foundation courses. A long time advocate of interdisciplinary courses for underclassmen, Soule had designed these courses as an alternative to either English 101 or English 102. However, although these courses involved a great deal of writing, usually a greater volume of writing than one generally completed in Introductory English, the focus of the courses was reading, writing, and discussion about "hot, current social issues," rather than composition.[29] Not only did students produce more pages of writing than they did in the Freshman English courses, but Law and Justice courses usually had rather demanding and challenging reading lists, containing work by such writers as Socrates, Martin Luther King, Jr., and Henry David Thoreau.

The Law and Justice courses were taught by faculty from the departments of English, Philosophy, Sociology, and History. Regarding theses courses, Soule explained, the great experimental question was, "Could faculty from other departments accomplish the aims of freshman composition?"[30] The faculty who volunteered to teach in this program thought they could do it, and Soule certainly hoped that they could. To facilitate this process, he not only organized and ran faculty development programming, but he also organized college-wide lectures on such topics as, "The Future of Interdisciplinary Courses and Programs: Problems and Possibilities."

In a late 1973 departmental response to a college level proposal that the interdepartmental freshman seminar program replace Freshman English, author Alan Paine, after consultation with Soule, withheld judgement until there was evidence that the Law and Justice courses satisfied the requirements of English 101 and 102. In this regard, history would show that, in spite of

Soule's faculty development efforts, the instructors from departments outside the English department never really learned how to respond to students' writing in a manner that was consistent with the development of introductory writing proficiency. In general, they were only able to comment on the content of students' work or their ability to argue logically.[31]

It is safe to say that had the interdisciplinary program satisfied the requirements of Freshman English, many on the full-time English faculty would have been greatly relieved, as the introductory program was growing much larger than the department could accommodate comfortably. In 1976, the freshman class numbered about 1150. Thus, the enrollment in English 101 was about 848, necessitating roughly 40 sections.[32] About 15 percent of the freshmen were enrolled in English 010 by virtue of their performance on a diagnostic writing sample administered during orientation.[33] An excerpt from a memo written by one professor captures the attitude of many full-timers regarding their responsibility for the introductory program, particularly remedial courses: "First, it appears that we will have too many freshman for our scheduled sections. Nothing is definite yet, but it may be necessary to cancel one or two advanced courses and replace them with you know what. Do I have any volunteers?"[34]

In spite of various college-level initiatives, the major responsibility for introductory instruction in composition never left the English Department. In 1976, when the Law and Justice courses had significant faculty support and interest, only about five percent of freshmen satisfied the writing requirement by taking these foundations courses.[35] By the late 1980s, this program was in jeopardy due to lack of faculty support. Perhaps, this drop off in interest was, at least in part, due to the fact that faculty were never successfully trained to respond to the aims and expectations of interdisciplinary courses in general, and Freshman English, in particular. Whatever the case, Soule acknowledged that he had doubts from the beginning about the possibility of a foundations course actually substituting for a section of Freshman English because, as was the case with the Great Books curriculum, "the emphasis had to be much more on the literature and interpretive abilities and critical reading."[36] Nevertheless, Soule believed that this interdisciplinary course was a good substitute for English 102 for many students who have learned to write competently in English 101 and could benefit from a second semester of coursework that involved using secondary sources in a challenging and relevant manner. This approach might, in fact, have been a very attractive alternative to those students who complain that the research component of English 102 seems tacked on and artificial; in Law and Justice courses, research was an integral part of an issue-oriented course.

Soule viewed his involvement in interdisciplinary curriculum development as part of the practical approach to public higher education advocated by then

President Stone. Unlike his predecessor, Bob Cooper, Soule was opposed to graduate studies at U.S.U., as well as "Ivy Tower assignments" and reading lists. He accepted the existence of a Masters level program in English only because it was described as being for teachers.[37] But, regardless of this difference of opinion regarding larger policy issues, these two men seemed to have little disagreement regarding the Freshman English program. Both men expressed a commitment to a bottom line of proficiency in writing, which included the mechanical skills cited in Cooper's 1975 statement of pedagogical objectives and minimum abilities.

Like Cooper, Soule pushed the department to require an exit examination for English 102. While much less disturbed by the anarchic nature of the freshman program than his predecessor, Soule believed that there had to be some degree of uniformity between sections of Introductory English. He proposed that the test serve the function of providing the professor with one more indicator to be used in the tabulation of final grades.[38] As tame as this proposition was, the majority of the faculty still viewed the exit exam as a violation of their exclusive right to evaluate student work.[39] Nevertheless, as Cooper had done the year before, Soule designed and administered a voluntary examination for English 102.

Soule's experience with the Law and Justice program was good preparation for the position of director of Freshman English because it required him to reflect upon the role of faculty development in instructional practice. This was a particularly important part of the director's job in 1976–77 because Colleges I and II had once again merged and it was necessary to develop a single Introductory English program, rather than two slightly different variations of courses.

Soule successfully encouraged the newly reunited staff to adopt a policy that required all instructors of English 102 to participate in small teaching groups (three to four members) during the Spring of 1977. These groups were to meet and agree on common objectives and techniques and some common materials and texts. Soule, along with Associate Chairman Matthew Gormley, tried to put together congenial groups that were to meet every week or two to review progress, discuss uniform standards, and plan assignments and future classes.[40]

The first obstacle Soule encountered in this faculty development initiative was that over half of the staff did not return their questionnaire regarding group selection before the textbook order deadline. Therefore, many instructors had to order books before they had selected membership in a teaching group. This left open the possibility that some people would be working in a group that was not congenial with text selection.[41]

In spite of this initial obstacle, Soule persisted in his plan to get all faculty meeting in small groups. Eventually, groupings were pieced together; however, the development of common curricula plans was limited as faculty continued both to create individual reading lists and stress different forms of skill building. Nevertheless, the groups did serve the function of bringing members of the two colleges together to discuss and consider some common principles for English 102. Although Phil Soule, like his predecessor, worked diligently to introduce a limited degree of uniformity in introductory curricula and instructional outcomes, his success in this area was quite limited. It was probably for this reason that he channeled most of his energies outside the department in the summer of 1977 when he took on the chairmanship of the College Committee for the Core Curriculum.

·7·

THE COMPETENCY-BASED CURRICULUM, 1977–1981

The present curriculum is deficient, lacking in a clear sense of goals, fragmented, failing to offer common educational experiences. . . . .There are doubts as to whether the departments' introductory courses support a meaningful phasing of education.
1977 COLLEGE CURRICULUM REVIEW COMMITTEE REPORT

As chairman of the College Committee for the Core Curriculum, Phil Soule worked to develop a revised, coherent curriculum, which was more than just a collection of courses derived from the merger of the two colleges. During the summer of '77, he provided leadership in the development of a new Core Curriculum that would have at its heart a combination of core courses and proficiency examinations in verbal and mathematical skills and foreign languages.[1] Within the Core Curriculum, all students would be required to take roughly one-third of their work as undergraduates in core courses; twelve courses would be chosen from two disciplinary areas (Foreign Languages and Mathematics and Computer Languages) and from five general areas (The Arts, Historical and Cultural Studies, Philosophical and Humanistic Studies, Social and Behavioral Sciences and Natural Sciences).

It was Soule's intention that the core courses provide undergraduates with Liberal learning, "the kind of learning that broadens awareness, deepens understanding, poses alternatives, and informs vital decisions."[2] Like many other academics across the country during this period, the faculty on the Curriculum Review Committee had come to realize that the requirement-free or "cafeteria style curriculum," as some cynically called it, had, for the most part, contributed to increased specialization on the part of undergraduates, rather than opening larger opportunities for self-directed studies. As was the case even at elite and innovative Brown University, left to their own initiative, students tended to skip over general education courses almost entirely, in favor of early specialization.[3]

The proposal for the New Curriculum was sent to the College of Arts and Sciences Senate in October of 1977. As was the case in the English Department, there was much debate over the notion of required proficiency testing, particularly examinations which had to be passed before students could assume upperclassman status.

Few faculty denied that U.S.U.'s undergraduates were poorly prepared for college work; but few could agree on what to do about this issue. Many faculty feared that proficiency examinations would make testing rather than instruction the primary focus of teaching. Others argued that the combination of three examinations would almost certainly serve to deny college degrees to a large group of minority and low-income students. Still others continued to argue that a student's course grade ought to be the sole indicator of competency.[4]

By May of 1978, when the dust had settled and the debates were finally over, the proposal that was approved included only a proficiency examination in writing. By a narrow margin, the senate voted to require students to write for two hours on one of three sets of readings in the Arts, the Natural Sciences, and the Social Sciences. The test would be given four times a year, and students could pick up packets of readings one month before the date of the examination.[5] The majority of faculty had come to an agreement with the Fundamental Skills Committee that all students enrolled in the College of Arts and Sciences should be proficient critical readers, writers and thinkers before they engaged in upper-level coursework. Across the nation during the 1970s, faculty came to similar decisions about accountability for proficiency in writing. In 1977, in response to faculty complaints that that the freshman writing program did not adequately prepare students for upper level assignments, the State University of New York, Stony Brook, put an examination of writing proficiency in place.[6] Likewise, in 1975, Eastern Oregon State College required that undergraduates pass a similar examination.[7] The University of Maryland, College Park, also instituted a writing proficiency requirement during this period; but this assessment took the form of an exit examination from Freshman English.[8]

As associate dean of the College of Arts and Sciences, Bob Cooper brought the Core into the college in the spring semester of 1979. The Core Curriculum was revised only slightly during the next two decades, with the addition of a diversity requirement and a few course inclusions and exclusions. An important aspect of this curriculum reform was the development of writing intensive "C" courses; these courses were offered in four of the distribution areas; the arts, historical and cultural studies, philosophical and humanistic studies, and social and behavioral sciences. Bruce Hamilton, who had taken on the directorship in the fall of 1977, became the first director of Freshman English to work within the context of this new curriculum.

The new curriculum did not diminish the significance of Freshman English; rather, this innovation reaffirmed the university's primary commitment to undergraduate instruction in writing. Although the required coursework included a package of distribution requirements that contained five writing intensive core or "C" courses, the only fixed requirement remained, "two courses (or demonstrated competence) in writing (grammar, rhetoric, and articulation of logical thought)."[9] However, it is important to note that by the early 1980s almost half of the undergraduates were transfer students.[10] Therefore, a significant percentage of students would have completed all or part of the Introductory English requirement elsewhere, most typically at a local community college. For those students who did not take English 101 and/or 102 at U.S.U., the "C" courses often represented their opportunity to develop the level of writing proficiency required for successful completion of both the writing examination and assignments in upper level courses.

At this point, one might be tempted to spend considerable time speculating about why, through all its reforms, U.S.U. remained so committed to writing instruction. Given that almost every other four-year liberal arts institution across the country maintained a similarly special place for freshman writing, the question becomes less interesting. However, at U.S.U. and peer institutions, such as the University of Maryland, College Park,[11] the need for composition instruction may have seemed even more pressing due to the belief among faculty that students were often so ill-prepared for college that their written work was all but incomprehensible. Surely, such a barrier to instruction was enough to cause many instructors to lobby for a significant commitment to writing instruction. Students may have been equally, or even more weak, in math and foreign languages, but such deficiencies were not immediately obvious and important to all faculty in all departments.

In *English in America*, Richard Ohmann maintains that Freshman English is a central course within the undergraduate curriculum because, "the values and folkways of Freshman English have important subterranean links to the values of industrial society."[12] The author argues that within this context the role of Introductory English is to teach students how to use language and literacy in ways that the dominant class in a capitalist society expects and needs in order to continue business as usual. Similarly, the current director of Freshman English maintains that much of traditional composition instruction and accompanying texts have a conservative social function in that students are expected to write in a manner that is skills-based and ahistorical. In her Introductory English classes, Parker has assigned Ohmann's book and asked students to revisit topic-based or thematic composition assignments from previous courses, locating their earlier writing in historical, social, and political contexts.

Ironically, although they might not agree with Ohmann's or Parker's philosophies regarding the purposes of Freshman English, many university administrators, such as former President Stone and former Chancellor Galvin, would have agreed with their premise that introductory curricula serves the needs of industry. For there have always been many involved with public higher education in this state who believe that the primary role of a public university is to benefit the state economy, while at the same time offering opportunities for upward mobility. In fact, one could argue that herein lies the tension surrounding the mission of state schools; on the one hand, scholars and statesmen such as Jefferson, Forester, and Reisman maintain that public universities should serve public, democratic ideals; while others, most recently including the current governor, believe that state schools should primarily serve private needs for economic success. This emphasis on individual rather than civic good moves the mission of state schools away from democratic, public goals and toward the needs of regional industries.

Whether it was to benefit the state, the economy or the frustrations of individual faculty members, all students who enrolled in the College of Arts and Sciences in or after the spring of 1979 were required to pass an examination of writing proficiency after they had accumulated 60 credits. Although all departments within the college assumed responsibility for administering, developing, and evaluating the examination, the English Department assumed more than its share of the work necessary for implementation.

The voluntary exit exam that Phil Soule developed for English 102 was the precursor to what was to become the required examination in writing proficiency.[13] This instrument, developed in 1976, contained four short common readings and some common essay questions. That Soule's test became the model for the Proficiency is not surprising, given his longstanding commitment to interdepartmental enterprises and the fact that he chaired the Summer Core Curriculum Committee.

Leigh Fields, wife of the first director of Freshman English and herself a part-time instructor of English, was primarily responsible for the development of *Nine Elements of Proficiency Writing*, a manual for students. In 1978, Bob Cooper asked Fields to work with a rough draft of the manual developed by a committee of faculty involved with the development of the Core Curriculum. Having been pieced together by a committee, rather than an individual, the draft Fields received suffered from unevenness and a lack of easy readability.[14] Hence, she found herself rewriting a good deal of the text, as well as adding new ideas to the manual itself. For instance, the committee had originally identified eight elements of good writing; however, Fields found that one of the elements was actually two elements, hence, the nine elements. The following are the nine elements which the committee and Leigh Fields found critical to writing proficiency:

1. Answer a question directly
2. Support your answer with clear, well-developed arguments
3. Show that you have read the source materials accurately
4. Define key terms when necessary
5. Focus on the intellectual issues in the question and avoid irrelevant digression into personal reminiscence or anecdote
6. Organize your argumentation in paragraphs
7. Use appropriate language
8. Use sentences with enough length and complexity to handle the subject matter and enough variety to hold the reader's attention
9. Abide by the rules of grammar and spelling[15]

The nine elements were a direct outgrowth of the minimum abilities identified by Bob Cooper during his first year as director of Freshman English. According to Cooper, without the manual detailing the nine elements, there could be no proficiency exam; for not only does the manual inform students of the specific composition skills on which they will be assessed, it also provides faculty with a specific checklist of criteria by which to evaluate the examinations. This standard created uniformity in grading and supplied a necessary support for faculty graders, particularly those from outside the English Department.[16] It is interesting to note that a quarter of a century later, in 2003, while the introductory curriculum had undergone extensive transformation, the nine elements remained as unchanged guidelines in the handbook for preparation for the examination.

By 1978, most members of the English Department felt they could support the proficiency examination because it was not viewed as an exit examination from English 102, but rather a test of a student's readiness to take on the writing challenges of upper level courses. Most English faculty could only accept an assessment that could not be interpreted as a check on their professional competence, such as the proficiency examination at the University of Maryland, College Park, which students completed as part of their introductory coursework. English Department faculty also responded favorably to the fact that the new curriculum required that all departments share the responsibility for instruction in writing across the curriculum.

Because preparation for the examination was not directly connected to a particular course or courses, the writing proficiency cannot technically be considered part of a competency-based approach.[17] As Levine notes, competency-based education consists of "learning experiences specifically designed to foster desired outcomes."[18] Few four-year colleges ever offer this type of curriculum, and of those that do, most have a strong professional orientation.[19] However, during the late 1970s and early 1980s, in the wake of a decade of openness characterized by few requirements, many college administrators, such as Soule and Cooper, were drawn to ideas that would renew a bottom-line standard of minimal proficiency within the undergraduate curriculum.[20]

Bruce Hamilton, director of Freshman English from 1977–81, originally had a college-level as opposed to department-level orientation toward the new curriculum. His experience implementing university-level policy was extensive. Prior to assuming the directorship, Hamilton had functioned as Assistant Chairman to Bob Cooper, Associate Provost, and, in 1976, Acting Provost. Also, interestingly enough, Hamilton was President of the University Senate at the time when the original Core Curriculum requirements were abolished in 1971.

To his credit, Hamilton did not allow his university-level orientation to lead him in the direction of making the Freshman Writing program a separate service department as it was at the flagship campus, and many other colleges and universities. According to him, this was due to the graduate training he received at Stanford in the late 1960s, which stressed the importance of Freshman English within the department.[21]

At Stanford, Hamilton had been enrolled in a semester-long course required of all potential TAs which focused on the instruction of Freshman English. This course was taught by the director of Freshman English who required that all students complete the course before entering a classroom as an instructor. This experience is somewhat similar to the one which graduate interns complete at U.S.U. Hamilton's thinking about the nature of the freshman course was greatly influenced by this form of teacher training. It was in this class that he first experienced group grading sessions, discussions of pedagogy, classroom observations, and review of instructional techniques. He claims that it was also in this course that he came to realize the importance of writing within the undergraduate curriculum. Here, Hamilton began to see a relationship between writing well and thinking well.

In the late 1980s, Hamilton claimed that the context of the position he inherited from Phil Soule had been basically defined by the work of Soule and Cooper, and his philosophy about what makes a good freshman course was primarily defined by his Stanford experience. He says of his predecessor that, "Soule developed a sense of identity with the institution among the part-timers and asserted a high quality of standards in teaching."[22] However, Hamilton maintained that he was able to institute several very important innovations during his four years as director. These included the establishment of a policy of annual review of part-time instructors, improved attendance at staff meetings, and the development of a program of faculty observing one another's classes.

During Hamilton's tenure as director, the percentage of part-timers teaching sections of Freshman English went as high as 75 percent.[23] This meant that not only did Hamilton have to engage in almost continuous interviewing and part-time recruitment, but he even had to keep the bookstore stocked with selections for generic sections of English 010, 101 or 102 which might not get authorized until the last minute due to the severe budget constraints of that era.

With so many part-timers, Hamilton ran the risk of losing all control over the content and quality of Freshman English. In order to avoid this fate, he instituted annual faculty reviews and scheduled at least one critical issue for consideration at each staff meeting. According to him, because issues of vital importance, rather than simply interesting discussion topics, were being decided at meetings, attendance went up. Increased attendance at staff meetings meant that Hamilton could communicate with and get to know instructors who might otherwise have quickly and quietly sailed on and off campus, stopping only long enough to teach their sections and hold the required office hour.

During meetings, Hamilton claims his primary goal was always, "to build a sense of common aim" which was compatible with the new curriculum. Basically he employed Bob Cooper's definitions of 010, 101, and 102 as well as the list of minimum abilities as a basis for discussion about what faculty should be accomplishing in their introductory sections.

Hamilton's policy of reviewing all part-timers annually translated into a major time commitment. This review, in part, was facilitated by his requirement that all faculty submit a complete course syllabus before the start of a given semester. This requirement not only all but eliminated the occasional practice of teaching a course week by week, but it also gave Hamilton a guideline for the faculty review. During reviews, he shared his own as well as student evaluations with the instructor, usually pointing out areas of strength as well as weakness, occasionally finding it necessary to tell someone that their work was not satisfactory.

From this director's perspective, the existence of the Writing Proficiency and the clearly articulated aims of the Core Curriculum clarified the work of the director; for, obviously, all faculty were now expected to teach the nine elements of good writing. Hamilton claims that, "by the time I became Director of Freshman English, there was fairly substantial agreement that some reference to the principles of composition expressed in rhetorical terms was important as a foundation for the curriculum. And that, in particular, a reference book for correct punctuation and other elements of style were important."[24] In contrast to this general trend, Hamilton notes that a few faculty espoused the theory that the complete methodology of the course ought to be based on the students' initial writing samples. These professors believed, not unlike Ohmann, that insistence on a rhetorical model was more likely to inhibit, rather than promote, the development of an authentic voice in any given student. Regarding the issue of writer's voice, it should be noted that the acquisition of "authentic voice" is not a minimal competency required for successful completion of the examination of writing proficiency, although many consider it an appropriate goal of Freshman English.[25]

As directors of Freshman English, both Bob Cooper and Phil Soule had struggled unsuccessfully to institute the sort of instructional bottom line that now was a mandated part of the curriculum. In providing support for the instruction of this minimum standard, Hamilton applied the lessons he had learned as a TA to his work in guiding instructors toward composition instruction that emphasized the nine elements and usually required a reference book for punctuation and the elements of style. He also tried, with only a limited degree of success, to get faculty to use at least one common text and attend colloquia on competency-based instruction.

Departmental data and recent interviews suggest that Hamilton was particularly good at accomplishing the ever-increasing managerial demands of the director's position. However, there are those among the faculty who insinuated that he provided minimal instructional leadership for full and part-time faculty. Rumors aside, it is true that most faculty interviewed do not mention Hamilton when asked to give a brief history of Introductory English. This does seem odd, given that he was the director for four years. On the other hand, maybe this omission is only a reflection of the low level of full-time faculty interest and involvement in the freshman curriculum during this period, rather than an expression of Hamilton's contribution to the curriculum.

·8·

TOWARD THE TWENTY-FIRST CENTURY, 1982–1990

I reject the caricature of the "hermetic" English department as a tomb in which literary high-priests worship the "sacred texts" of an embalmed literary canon while they treat their students' writing as pseudo-texts worthy only of product-oriented editing or else relegate those pseudo-texts to the ministrations of composition teachers, usually the sacrificial vestal virgins of academe.

EMILY JONES, DIRECTOR OF FRESHMAN ENGLISH, 1987

When Joyce Campbell became the first chairwoman of the English Department in 1982, she brought a strong commitment to instruction in composition to this position, as well as an equally strong dedication to affirmative action. It had been years, decades really, since her first semester at Urban State when she had rejected the practice of a product-oriented response to student work and the notion of professor as high priest, or even priestess. For both these reasons, she asked Emily Jones if she would be interested in becoming the next director of the introductory program. This invitation was a bold move, given that Jones held only a five-sixths fractional faculty appointment. After she agreed to her proposal, Campbell presented Jones's name to the Executive Committee. In 1982, Emily Jones assumed the directorship.[1]

At Urban State, particularly in the English Department, Jones's appointment was a rather unique event. In general, after 1970, a part-time position, even a fractional assistant or associate professorship, was the kiss of death as far as advancement within the department was concerned. Women were especially likely to become caught up in years, sometimes decades, of this low-paid service-oriented work which seldom offered them health or other benefits. Jones, mother of two and wife of English Professor Albert Jones, became one of the few exceptions to this rule when she moved from her fractional appointment to a full-time position as director of Freshman English.

There were those among the old-timers who did not feel that Jones was the person for the job. As an untenured, former part-timer, she had limited control over the curricula of the full-timers who still taught roughly one fourth of the freshman courses.[2] For example, former director, David Fields, declared that he would not go along with Jones's expectation that all sections of English 102 include a research paper. He maintained that her expectations did not constitute department requirements.[3] Other full-timers, confident that it was not their job to teach freshmen how to write lengthy research papers, also rebelled, or simply ignored Jones's guidelines regarding this assignment.

Fields, like several other full-timers, felt that Jones was too conservative in her approach to curricula. He disagreed with what he saw as her emphasis on structured, traditional approaches to assigned work, epitomized by the research paper.[4] Jones's only real option was to ignore the grumbling and prerogatives of these old-timers. Some faculty mentioned that this lack of power over tenured full-timers is one reason why a relatively inexperienced faculty member should not be the director of a major program; however, in this regard, it is important to remember that even faculty as powerful as former department chairs Cooper and Soule had limited success enforcing compliance with their instructional and curriculum guidelines.

In reality, Jones was relatively successful in her attempts to guide curriculum development and instruction because she had the respect of many long time faculty, including Mark Franklin, who succeeded Campbell as department head.[5] In fact, it may be that Jones's conservatism, more accurately described as a competency building orientation, permitted this former part-timer to be taken seriously when the opinions of others, particularly women, of similar status and/or experience were often trivialized or ignored.

Dr. Campbell believed that Jones's experience as supervisor and director of the tutoring program as well as her extensive knowledge of composition theory more than made up for the few negatives that came with her relatively low status within the department. Campbell's frustration with the status of women faculty members at U.S.U. must also have contributed to her desire to see a woman in the director's position. In this regard, it seems highly likely, given her admiration for the curriculum theories and educational philosophy of her longtime friend and colleague, Ann Roberts, that Campbell might have recruited her to the directorship if she had not been denied tenure at U.S.U. during the early 1970s.

Like so many other academics that received their PhDs in English during or after the early seventies, Jones had little teaching experience in the area of her dissertation, the late 18th century Romantic period. At the time that she assumed the directorship, it was unlikely that she would teach courses in this area until at least the early 1990s when those who had seniority in this area might retire. As she and many others of her generation tell it, "composition theory and instruction was what there was" by the time they were looking for employment.[6]

Before coming to U.S.U. in 1974, Jones taught composition at a traditionally Black college in the South, as well as a compensatory education program at a large university in the northeast. Both these positions provided the future director with experience working with student populations similar to those found at U.S.U. i.e., minorities, adult learners, urban populations and underprepared students.

Prior to her 1982 appointment as director, Jones combined teaching at U.S.U. with another part-time position teaching in a prison.[7] This meant that her so-called part-time employment involved teaching The Seminar for Tutors, supervising tutorial work, teaching freshman composition, and instructing prisoners to write competently. During this period, Jones appears to have had little time for Romantic literature. However, unlike most part-timers who often stagnate intellectually under the burden of multiple class preparations, she was able to publish and present numerous lectures and articles relevant to composition theory and writing-across-the-curriculum. Perhaps her most important contribution in this area was the publication of a text, which Jones co-authored with the co-instructor of The Seminar for Tutors. This text details their experiences teaching upperclassmen how to teach writing, particularly remedial writing, to their peers. This book became a popular handbook for faculty and administrators who wanted to implement peer support in introductory classes.

Unlike the previous directors of the freshman program, Jones came to her position as someone who had spent almost all of her professional life immersed in issues relevant to the curriculum of Freshman English. For this reason, while some faculty may have felt she lacked credibility as a literary scholar, she became the director with the deepest background in the analysis of instructional methodology and curriculum development. This experience allowed her to move far beyond the management-oriented issues of minimum course requirements and minimum abilities and into explorations of more subtle considerations relevant to the instruction of freshman courses. Accordingly, she functioned increasingly as a college-level resource person, advising faculty outside the English Department how to integrate meaningful writing assignments into their Core courses.[8]

The major focus of Jones's first year in the director's position had to be the university's merger with the local state teacher's college. This reorganization strategy on the part of a newly formed state board had major ramifications within the English Department, as well as the rest of the university. In the late spring of 1982, in anticipation of the merger, all part-time faculty were told that they would no longer have a job at the end of the academic year. Then, in the summer, everyone was offered his or her job back.[9] Many valued and experienced part-timers decided that it was too risky to work at Urban State and decided not to return. This meant that Campbell and Jones had to spend most of the summer of '82 putting together a part-time faculty adequate to meet the expanded demands of the introductory program that would now have to serve a new population of students.[10]

At the teacher's college, the introductory curriculum had consisted of one semester of composition and one semester of introduction to literature. The faculty who were now part of the English Department by virtue of the merger were generally pleased that they would be working with a curriculum that included two semesters of instruction in writing. Many had found that their students increasingly required an extra semester of practice in writing. Like the U.S.U. faculty of the sixties, these faculty found that the study of literature took up time that they wanted to devote to writing instruction. Additionally, several faculty indicated that the students brought into the university by the merger were on average less proficient in writing than the typical U.S.U. undergraduate.

After the merger, the eight-year-old Oceanside campus had a full house. Dr. Jones was responsible for directing roughly 80 sections of Freshman English (including English as a Second Language) per semester. This meant that, including summer school, 4,000 students took Introductory English that year.[11]

By 1982, the director of Freshman English had become almost more central to the functioning of the College than she was to the department. By that time, the position required about a 50–50 split between department and college level business.[12] This situation was a result of the regulations governing the new Core Curriculum which required that the director be a permanent member of the Fundamental Skills Committee which designed the Writing Proficiency Examinations, ran the holistic Proficiency grading sessions, and contributed to any committee dealing with the requirement that students attain writing proficiency. Therefore, Jones was often out of the department attending meetings, seminars, and conferences concerned with issues ranging from freshmen orientation to retention to testing to public school liaison projects. This experience undoubtedly laid the groundwork for her eventual appointment as Acting Dean of the College of Arts and Sciences two decades after she became Director of Freshman English.

The director's work in the department centered on teaching the course for tutors, supervising tutor work with peers and interactions with faculty, and interviewing, reviewing, and advising part-time faculty. The demands on her time in the department increased during the mid-1980s when budget constraints required the elimination of the position of associate director. According to Jones, her largest block of time, both before and after the elimination of the associate position, went to, "basically helping people with the daily teaching that goes on," rather than designing a program as Bob Cooper had done.

In an effort to systematize her program of faculty development and support, Jones instituted a colloquium series aimed at exploring issues relevant to Introductory English. This program ran for several years until 1985 when the graduate program in English began a series that included many topics relevant to introductory instruction. The speakers in Jones's program were usually members of the college faculty, but the series, somewhat similarly to the meetings organized by Director Paine in the early 1970s, occasionally featured experts in the fields of composition theory and instructional methodology for adult learners.

For someone who is often described by her peers as conservative, Jones's reaction to the unstructured, once considered anarchic, freshman curriculum seems surprising. "Some might describe it as anarchy," said she, "but I think it's a good thing." Therefore, unlike former directors Paine and Hamilton, Jones never attempted to institute common texts. While she was quick to point out that this arrangement should not be interpreted to mean that all curricula are equally good (she discouraged the instruction of imitation of rhetorical models, for example); Jones was very open to most innovations suggested by the freshman staff. For example, when one part-timer said she wanted to design a freshman course around six books about women and work, Jones's response was "Wow. Let's see how we can make that work."

Jones acknowledged that her flexible attitude toward curricula would not work everywhere, and maintained that she would run the program very differently if the staff consisted of TAs or inexperienced instructors. She was quick to point out that by the 1980s most part-timers were seasoned college instructors. The majority of these people had clearly defined areas of expertise and interest, many having publications and presentations on their resumes. At one point in the early 1980s, in an attempt to make the administration aware of the quality of the part-time staff, Jones conducted a survey to determine the number of doctorates held by instructors of writing and presented her "impressive findings" to the Dean.

Jones was very sensitive to the fact that the tight job market for people with graduate degrees in the Liberal Arts meant that many part-time instructors would never have the opportunity to teach genre courses in the area of their specialization. Therefore, she supported and encouraged their natural inclinations to develop introductory curricula relevant to their areas of specialization.

Because the freshman staff was so well qualified, really overqualified, for the positions they held, Jones felt that half her time and their time would be taken up with intradepartmental feuding if she attempted to tell them what to teach, or even specifically how to teach. Therefore, she chose to "find out what each faculty member is interested in, so they can use their interests and expertise to accomplish the goals of the course."[13] Jones felt quite strongly that "it would be boring to have everything canned." She believed that the diversity of the introductory curriculum was one of its strongest features, for both students and faculty.

It is interesting to speculate why, given her flexible attitude toward curricula, anyone would describe Emily Jones as conservative. One can only speculate that this image was a function of her no-nonsense style and her repeated objection to therapeutic approaches to instruction, as well as "soft," 1960s' style grading standards.[14] Regarding the later, this Director often told part-timers not to give Ds as good conduct awards. Her directions in this regard were, "If someone is flunking, give them an F." Such directives, coupled with a clear objection to highly personalized approaches to instruction, appear to have caused some old-timers to view Jones as rigid and conservative. In this regard, it is also possible that her attitude rubbed old wounds raw; for there were those among the faculty who were still full of despair over the dreams and educational experiments deferred in the early 1970s. Some of them responded defensively to the director's advice against "sixties' softness."

Jones' course guidelines for all sections of Freshman English can fit on two pieces of paper. They were basically Bob Cooper's list of minimal abilities, supplemented by a few paragraphs that detailed the rationale for selecting these particular competencies ("For we find our fundamental concern throughout the year must be with clear and effective word usage and sentence form.").[15]

Aside from reviewing the goals for introductory courses with new faculty, Jones typically reviewed a paper set with new and inexperienced instructors to insure that they led students toward course goals, that their grades were consistent with departmental standards, and that their paper comments were useful, i.e., no more than two or three clearly and positively cited problems per paper.[16]

Although Emily Jones was proud of the quality of the part-time staff she supervised, she believed that their low status kept them from making the kinds of contributions that they were capable of making to the students and the college. In 1985, part-timers had gone without a raise since 1974; therefore, most worked two, three, sometimes even four other jobs. Efforts at getting health benefits for part-timers had repeatedly failed, and many instructors found that they had to pay as much as $2000 per year for private coverage for themselves and their dependents. These factors often contributed to burnout and feelings of low self-worth.

Because Jones felt so strongly about the conditions of the part-timers, she spent a significant amount of time during 1984–85 involved in preparing a report on the status of part-timers at Urban State University. As someone who once described herself as "part-time forever," Jones was motivated by strong feelings about the university's relationship with its expanding part-time faculty.[17]

In a 1987 interview, Jones departed briefly from her usual understated style when she spoke of the committee that was created to put together the report concerning the status of part-timers. After the first meeting in the fall of 1984, the administrative representatives never again attended a scheduled meeting. Although the faculty representatives resented this lack of involvement on the part of the administration, they nevertheless went ahead and conducted the study without their participation.[18]

The October 1985 memo to all faculty detailing the faculty response to the study is of interest for a variety of reasons. Aside from the absence of administrative imput, one is immediately impressed with the fact that of the three authors of the study, two have held the position of director of Freshman English. While at first this may seem inexplicable, given that U.S.U. employed 350 part-timers by 1985, it makes some sense that these two faculty members would be most concerned about the status and role of part-timers when the success of the university's largest introductory program was so dependent upon the quality of instruction delivered by part-time instructors.[19]

The general tone of this report on the status of part-timers is one of deep concern and alarm over the increased reliance on "the new migrant or gypsy faculty" at U.S.U., as well as other schools throughout the country.[20] The authors noted that national surveys during 1985 indicated that part-timers often constituted 30 percent to 40 percent of university or college faculties. In brief, the committee recommended that part-time faculty who had not received a raise from $1,500 per course since 1974 (during a period when full-time salaries almost doubled) be granted an immediate pay increase and some fringe benefits, and that the University "foster ways to bind part-time faculty more closely to it" by involving these instructors in advising and departmental committee work, as well as providing compensation and opportunities for research and other scholarly endeavors."[21]

Not only did Emily Jones and former director Bob Cooper share concerns about the status and role of part-timers, but they also shared a long-standing commitment to lowering the level of attrition in introductory courses. In the document concerning part-timers, they allude to a possible connection between "temporary faculty and temporary students"; and during interviews, they, as well as several other faculty, spoke with strong emotions about the problem of "disappearing students" at this urban commuter college.[22]

Regarding attrition, Cooper observed, in the late 1980s, that the student disappearances didn't follow any pattern that made sense to him; an enthusiastic A student was just as likely to drop out as is the indifferent C- student. He claimed that these losses had a major effect on faculty; they tended to question the meaning and value of their work when significant numbers of students stopped attending classes.[23]

In the early 1980s, Emily Jones attempted to combat the extreme rate of absenteeism in most sections of English 102. Despairing faculty, both full and part-timers, complained that it was not unusual for a class of 24 to contain less than ten or eight students on any given day.[24] This pattern of attendance made consistent and meaningful instruction almost impossible. Hence, Jones held meetings in which faculty swapped strategies for obtaining improved attendance. As a function of this type of discussion, many faculty began to experiment with attendance policies for Introductory English, something that was all but unheard of during the late sixties and early seventies when most faculty were strongly influenced by the prevailing policy of personal choice and freedom for students.

Several faculty, particularly some of the old timers, speculate that the research component of English 102 drove busy working students away from the classroom.[25] Others speculate that students were simply tired of Freshman English by the time they got to the second semester.[26] Some speculated that the problem of attrition was simply an extension of a larger attendance problem that plagued urban public schools. In a recent 2002 interview, a current transfer student spoke of her shrinking Freshman English class in a manner that mirrored observations made by others twenty years earlier.[27] However, in the more recent case, the rate of absenteeism can not be attributed to exhaustion over a second semester of Introductory English; as transfer students with an average of over 40 credits, the majority of undergraduates no longer took English 101 in the College of Arts and Sciences.[28] In fact, by the fall of 1984, the number of transfer students exceeded the number of first time freshmen; the percentage of transfer students has only continued to climb over time.[29] Senior Jake Stein who transferred credits from four different colleges at the time of his matriculation to Urban State remarked that, "it's impossible to find a place to park at the beginning of a semester but after a few weeks, a lot of kids leave and there are plenty of spaces."[30] Certainly some students must leave while they can still get a refund on tuition; but Stein echoes the observations of faculty when he says that there seems to be no particular pattern to the attrition. Whatever the causes of low attendance in Introductory English, instructors continue to discuss attendance policies, missed assignments, and what to do about those confusing, semi-research papers from students who haven't attended class for weeks.

By the early 1980s, some faculty began to view problems with reading as one of the major causes of low writing proficiency and attrition. In this regard, they shared a perspective and a concern with many in the field of education across the nation. In 1983, the National Commission on Excellence in Education published *A Nation at Risk*, a report documenting a decline in America's secondary schools. Among the report's findings, there was much that had relevance for college faculty, particularly those involved with the instruction of undergraduate introductory courses. According to the Commission, 23 million Americans were illiterate and only a fifth of 17-year-olds could write a persuasive essay.[31]

In the November, 1983 issue of *Educational Researcher*, the late Jeanne Chall, a highly regarded reading expert, explored the trend toward lower rates of literacy among high school and college students, particularly those from low income groups. Many of these students had relatively good achievement in the early grades; but their reading levels fell throughout their time in middle school, high school, and college. Chall theorizes that an emphasis, or rather overemphasis, on basic skills during the early 1970s may have produced a generation of young people who had been overtaught the basics, and not sufficiently exposed to higher-level literacy skills.[32]

Chall, Jacobs, and Baldwin's 1990 research finding that both above-average and below-average low-income child readers had consistently low scores on understanding of word meaning further explains the reading and writing deficiencies of underprepared college students.[33] The gap between the vocabulary development of these children and their higher income peers consistently widened as students progressed through grade four and beyond. This elementary school shift in the achievement of low-income children has the potential to effect the content area reading that students are assigned throughout high school and into college. In general, by grade four, children are presented with textbooks containing abstract technical and literary terminology, as well as expository prose. For low-income students, who often do not have the benefit of at-home fluency lessons, an overreliance on decoding and one-dimensional word recognition strategies can function as a barrier to learning how to read complicated expository texts.

Most of the national reports written during the early and middle eighties support Chall's findings. They indicate that a reliance on packaged, highly structured educational programs (workbooks, worksheets, anthologies, textbooks and readers) during the 1970s lead to a decline in the kinds of literacy skills one can only acquire from reading and reflecting upon something long and hard, in other words, a challenging book. This form of back-to-basics instruction is also more than likely somewhat responsible for the noted increase in the type of student whom Phil Soule described as, "a competent writer with absolutely nothing to say."[34]

Because attention was beginning to be paid to the issue of reading, books, rather than readers and anthologies, were put back into the curriculum of Introductory English by the mid-1980s. In 1982, as Department Chair, Dr. Campbell advised me and other newly hired part-timers to assign the *Little Brown Handbook* and "some sort of reader." She supported her case for the reader with statements about the lack of time for literature and the need to channel most of one's instructional efforts into the instruction of writing. By 1984, Emily Jones encouraged most of her faculty to assign whole books to freshmen; and, once again, after almost two decades of focusing on composition instruction, training in reading began to have a place in some sections of English 101 and 102.[35]

During faculty interviews, almost all faculty indicated that they had not read any of the national reports on the status of higher education published in the 1980s. A few mentioned reading, or reading about, William Bennett's *To Reclaim a Legacy*. Therefore, it makes no sense to attribute the renewed interest in reading instruction to these reports. Rather, it appears that student performance on the proficiency examination in writing was the major factor contributing to this increased attention to reading comprehension. However, the fact that student performance indicated problems in reading comprehension does support the accuracy of the reports' findings.

By the early 1980s, several full-timers who were committed to freshman instruction used old copies of writing proficiency reading packages to teach critical reading skills. By the late 1980s, Laura Cormack stressed that her course was really an introduction to college-level reading, writing, and thinking, rather than an English course per se. Hence, she assigned texts and copied articles from the various disciplines represented by the readings in the Proficiency Exam.

Even the grumblings heard in the halls during the middle and late 1980s frequently focused on the topic of reading and college students. Many faculty were becoming aware that significant numbers of students suffered due to problems with literacy. Frequently, this meant that they could not keep up with assignments, or they feared being asked to read aloud in class, or misinterpreted written directions and questions.

When it became apparent that a misreading of the assigned question was the number one reason for failure on the Proficiency Exam, many faculty began to take a serious look at both the questions and the readings.[36] Subsequently, several faculty felt that the content of the selections was often inappropriate for the hard-hat crowd who frequently had little experience with literature in the social or hard sciences. Such faculty theorized that while students might be able to read at the level in which such articles were written, they did not have the background knowledge to comprehend them. By the mid-1980s, the majority of students were transfer students; therefore, the college now had both less control over and knowledge of the content of introductory instruction.

As mentioned previously, I returned to my alma mater in 1982 as a part-time instructor of Introductory English. Ironically, I found myself teaching courses in which, as part of the earlier Great Books curriculum, I had once struggled to earn passing grades. At that time, many students in the College of Arts and Sciences were intimidated by the requirement that they complete the writing proficiency before advancing in their undergraduate careers. Not wanting to replicate the 1960s' climate of confusion and failure, I was determined to teach a course that was challenging enough to prepare students for the level of reading and writing required by the proficiency and compelling enough to motivate students to engage with assignments that prepared them for advanced college work. To do this, I drew upon my background as a K-12 teacher in the development of a literature-based course that focused on real people and fictional characters grappling with a host of issues associated with growing up in poverty in America. Thinking like a whole language teacher[37] in a college setting was not an enormous leap for someone who had experienced this institution's original curriculum. I even discovered that some faculty were still teaching modifications of the Great Books course successfully.

I took advantage of the freedom offered to part-timers and developed introductory courses with readings that focused on a range of themes that I thought would appeal to the wide age range (approximately 16–55 years) found in introductory courses at that time. By the late 1980s, I had developed a section of English 102 that was designed around readings describing and/or depicting children growing up below the median income. This course contained writing assignments designed to accommodate most learning styles reflected in a college classroom that included so-called at-risk students. The research papers written by those students offer insights into both student voices and the effectiveness of drawing upon student interest in the "helping" professions as a strategy for instruction in the development of writing skills needed for advanced college work. For example, one young man wrote, "I would like to help Willie Lee from the story 'Requiem for Willie Lee.' This young man is what most people would simply call a waste; a waste of human potential and of being. He is a mass of undisciplined, unmotivated reckless energy who has hardly been given any help or supervision during his life." Another student wrote, "Mr. Allesandro has my full sympathy not only because he's homeless but because of who he is, his character. He is a decent man who cares deeply for his children and shows great admiration and respect for his mother. The values that Mr. Allesandro possesses are those which I strive for myself in my daily life." While the student writing reveals some technical weaknesses, the voices are generally honest and authentic, indicating that students not only understood why they were conducting research, but also felt engaged in the process. Particularly compelling is my recollection of a young man, a proud conservative, who believed that Kozol's *Rachel and Her Children* was a literary fabrication. He went to New York to see if the hotel where the homeless lived existed. "It's worst than Kozol described," he told the class upon his return. For him, the "helping" assignment in which students researched their character's problem and/or condition (child abuse, domestic violence, homelessness, addiction, etc.) became both an academic and personal turning point; thus, accomplishing one of the primary goals of general education.

Belanoff notes that working and lower-middle-class students tend to exhibit "the most language insecurity" and are most likely to "adjust their language toward the formal."[38] Hence, the type of engagement experienced by the student who researched the authencity of Kozol's work is particularly important for members of the hard-hat crowd who are trained to give parents, teachers, bosses, clergy, or other authority figures, "what they want." Like Belanoff, almost all who study underprepared college students acknowledge this socialization process and the role it plays in maintaining the status quo and silencing working class expression, yet few academics consider that their students are responding to them as they would to any authority figure. It is painful to recollect how my classmates and I once pretended to "learn" something we already knew or a point of view it was clear the professor wanted us to acquire. Success in college, we assumed, required that we acquire both the language and the perspectives of our professors. We often joked about this game over coffee at the end of the day; but I now cringe at those memories. Genuine learning can not occur when students misrepresent their voice, knowledge or beliefs.

After teaching Freshman English for several years, I received a memo from the director to all instructors of English 102. The memo explained that there was "going to be a court case in which the university may have to demonstrate that it prepares students well for the Writing Proficiency Exam." The memo concluded with a sign-up form for a multisectioned Writing Proficiency Examination exercise using common readings and anonymous grading. Through the campus rumor mill, I heard that some students had gone to the Office of Civil Rights to complain that the requirement that students pass the examination before proceeding past 60 credits was a violation of the civil rights of second language learners. As the memo predicted, the university did come under the observation of the Office of Civil Rights but there was no finding. In the early 1990s, the case was reopened, and at that time the university was found to be in compliance.

My recent conversations with faculty, administrators and alumni at the university reveal few recollections of this suit. The current director of The Writing Proficiency Program recalled that the original suit did seem to lead to "a lot of scurrying around" to upgrade the quality of the writing-intensive intermediate courses offered within the Core Curriculum, as well as the inclusion of more multicultural readings within the reading sets for the proficiency examination.[39]

There is speculation that this civil rights case was reopened through the efforts of a faculty member who was strongly opposed to the examination. But, most questions about this issue meet with silence and forgetfulness. Little wonder. The subject of the education of recent immigrants strikes at the heart of the school's original mission to "seek out and support those young people whose race, or recent immigration, or depressed economic status denies them higher education." Most long time faculty and recent retirees insist that this mission remains basically unchanged; legal action that symbolizes a denial of this mission is undoubtedly too painful to contemplate or even remember.

In 1989, Jones left the position of director of Freshman English for a year's sabbatical. The new director, Deborah Parker, was already a recognized scholar in the field of composition theory.

Upon her return from sabbatical in 1990, Emily Jones became editor-in-chief of a journal dedicated to the study of instruction in English. At the century's end, Jones transitioned from this position to the chairmanship of the English Department. Once "part-time forever," she had come a long way.

·9·

JOINT CUSTODY, 1990–2003

"Start with the reality that this university has already changed. What we need to do now is get enough in control of that change so that we can preserve as much of what we have built over the past 25 years."

U.S.U. PROVOST

By the 1990s, three powerful real-world factors dramatically affected the curriculum of Introductory English; they were the decline in state funding, increases in the cost of tuition and fees, and declining numbers of first time freshmen. All three were and continue to be interrelated, and result in increasing declines in the percentage of students in the College of Arts and Sciences who received credit for English 101 and English 102 at this urban campus. By 1990, less than 40 percent of the students enrolled in CAS took both sections of this introductory general education requirement at U.S.U. Hence, from this point in time, the particular curriculum that is the focus of this study plays a less significant role in the education of the hard-hat crowd. This situation is ironic in that this period also coincides with a time in the College when a quartet of literacy experts collaborated on the creation of introductory courses that were informed by engagement with both international theoretical perspectives on literacy learning and innovations in K-12 Language Arts instruction.

As was the case across the nation, the northeastern states were well into education reform by the last decade of the 20th century. Beginning in 1983 with the publication of *A Nation at Risk* and its subsequent soundbites that echoed across the land in the mouths of politicians and talk-show hosts, Americans became increasingly negative about and unsupportive of public education. In this state, where middle class residents had a long history of preferring private over public postsecondary education, the public colleges and universities suffered from an increasing lack of taxpayer support in spite of regional reports issued earlier in the decade linking access to higher education to economic growth.[1] As recently as the 2003–2004 academic year, appropriations for the state university system were down by a double-digit number.[2]

As part of this era of reform, the various report cards issued by the Reagan and Bush administrations exerted pressure on public schools to assume business models of accountability. Generally opposed to a product or outcomes-based orientation toward instruction, most academics responded negatively to pressure for assessment or skills-driven models of teaching. While it was one thing for the founder of a fast food chain to keep his eyes on the bottom line, few American educators viewed schools as compatible with one-size-fits-all criteria for achievement. "Keep it simple stupid," perhaps a useful philosophy for MacDonald's, had little attraction for educators, especially academics who are trained to value the complex, complicated, analytical, and creative. In particular, assessment that primarily measured mastery of standard English and/or cultural literacy met with significant opposition from faculty who were often involved in a range of campus-wide multicultural education initiatives. In fact, by the 1990s, a diversity requirement became a new graduation requirement at U.S.U., one that appeared to balance the potential for cultural bias inherent in the writing proficiency requirement. Similar new multicultural requirements were common at colleges and universities nationwide during this period of otherwise limited curricular change.[3] Statewide reform efforts culminated in tests that affected public school students in kindergarten through college. Children in fourth, eighth and tenth grades began sitting through days of testing in core subjects, while college students preparing to teach were required to take tests that primarily assessed their background in literacy and the liberal arts, as opposed to pedagogy or child development. While some educators welcomed the examinations as an opportunity to underscore the value of a particular skill set, many complained that the assessment was now driving curriculum.

During the early 1990s, still committed to the idea of "equity in curriculum substance," the first dean of CAS went to Washington as the head of a foundation dedicated to the improvement and reform of teaching. His office funded an initiative that led to the development of national standards, as opposed to national assessment. But, he said recently, except for the civics standards, "they are miserable failures." The final document was not a usable guide for educators as it was over 1,000 pages long, containing all that everyone involved thought was important. The educators that Millet recruited ignored his charge to use the work of countries with centralized educational systems as guidance in crafting a list of essential knowledge and standards. According to him, they could not make choices about curriculum standards or essential knowledge, so the work was turned over to the states. In the mid-

1990s, resolute in his half-century-old mission to create equitable academic standards, the elderly first dean, in collaboration with a national teacher union leader, studied the relative effectiveness of the new state standards in preparing democratic citizens. They found that even those states that were relatively successful in creating workable standards still had too much content and plenty of discontinuity.

As mentioned in Chapter 7, Dr. Deborah Parker who assumed the directorship of Freshman English at a time when the public favored accountability for most things educational, is critical of approaches to the acquisition of college level literacy that define successful instruction as coursework leading to the attainment of a particular skill or knowledge set. This director emphasizes that the meaning and value of particular forms of reading and writing are not timeless, but rather contingent on history.[4] Parker's scholarship indicates that she is aware that many of the writing proficiencies emphasized by the introductory English curriculum could be viewed as simply serving the status quo as understood by groups such as the National Alliance of Business which emphasized in its 2000 report that the future of the nation's economy depended upon, "how broadly and deeply Americans reach a new level of literacy—21st-century literacy—that includes strong academic, thinking, reasoning, and teamwork skills, and proficiency in using technology."[5] In contrast to this marketization of literacy, Parker's composition theory emphasizes that competency in language use is merely the beginning of a process. In the First Year Writing Outcomes Statement, which is strongly influenced by the director, there is an emphasis on "entry-level critical literacy" that should function as a foundation for advanced literacy. Here, we see that while the introductory competencies developed in Freshman English may be compatible with the needs of business, they are not ends in themselves. It is a clear goal of the first year writing program that students reflect on the purposes of language use, and develop their own voice as they evolve as readers and writers.

The tension between the interests of business and those of academe have always been part of the life of this university; this is implicit in the very nature of public higher education, but it is particularly powerful at Urban State University. In the 1960s, the president of the state senate invoked the needs of a fast-growing economy to garner the votes needed for the creation of the urban campus; but within years of passing the bill that created this school, the business community organized to relegate the university's permanent location to the city's margins. In the the 1960s, academics Millet and Sheehan responded to a national climate of competition with the USSR with assertions of the value of a traditional knowledge base as the best guardian of democracy. When David Fields became the first director of Freshman English in 1968, he oversaw a program in which most of the instructors where full-time faculty, as compared to the 1990s when most sections were taught by adjuncts or graduate students.

In the 1980s and 1990s, many academics at Urban State and elsewhere were drawn to the scholarship of liberation as advocated by Freire and Giroux. Such scholarship underscores the class bias of skills-based instruction, advocating an instructional approach that transforms relationships between students and teachers through the creation of discourse communities in which readers and writers perceive the historical and social origins of literacy and language.[6] While seemingly unaware of Freire's work, Paine and Skye were teaching in a manner that was consistent with that advocated by Freire and Giroux when they team-taught their conversation-based course described in Chapter 5. In fact, a review of faculty seminars sponsored by U.S.U.'s center for teaching improvement during the 1990s indicates that Paine's earlier efforts to transform teacher-centered instruction were now realized in the faculty with a strong preference for professional development focusing on the learning needs of diverse populations. Topics such as "Teaching about Diversity in Introductory Classes" and "Inclusive Teaching and Academic Standards: Challenges and Opportunities" had many participants.

By the mid-1970s, the postwar era boom that birthed this public university was over; downsizing was the trend both in business and allocations to public higher education.[7] In 1975, confronted with a $350 million budget deficit, a liberal governor called upon the legislature to "make a Herculean effort to reduce expenditures"; one result was a reduction in funds for education.[8] Some thirty years later, in the face of what he interpreted as low retention and graduation rates, a conservative governor made front page news with his proposal to restructure state colleges with greater emphasis on job training that was compatible with the needs of area businesses. By the end of 2003, this governor proposed tying the budgets of state colleges and universities to their performance on easily measured criteria, such as graduation rates, tuition increases, and ease of transfer. In response to such recommendations, the president of the state university system accused the governor of "class warfare." Within the College of Arts and Sciences, a similar tension existed between those with a practical orientation to introductory instruction and those faculty who, while valuing the attainment of writing proficiency, believed their primary responsibility was the creation of discourse communities. Those who sought to transform their classrooms into learning communities viewed instruction in both introductory and advanced writing as much more complicated than the filling of empty (student) vessels, and certainly more than teaching that would produce students who could write competently in business settings.

In a 1990 university planning report, the chancellor acknowledged that, "given the drastic reduction of state funding during the last two years, it is not possible for the campus to maintain the current level of academic and support services in their present configuration."[9] One result of this new round of cuts in state funding was additional increases in the cost of attending the university. Hence, by the last decade of the century, roughly two thirds of the students in the College of Arts and Sciences were transfer students who generally received credit for Introductory English at less expensive "feeder" schools, most typically local community colleges. With the freshman yield at 612 in the fall of 1990, U.S.U. needed the 1,013 transfer students it would also admit,[10] and transfer students were eager to attend as soon as they had received their general education credits in a cost-effective manner. Across the nation, by the 1990s, increasing numbers of graduates of state universities, similarly burdened by rising tuition, began their undergraduate careers at less expensive community colleges.[11]

One might assume that the above state of affairs would lead to simplified or minimalistic approaches to teaching Freshman English. But ironically, the same political and economic realities that led to budget-slashing and tuition and fee increases also coincided with a period of serious study of introductory writing instruction among a generation that knew better than to pin their academic futures on study of Beowolf or Wordsworth. Nationally, by century's end, those who came to assume positions of leadership in the field of Freshmen English, such as Mike Rose at the University of California at Los Angeles, came increasingly from the ranks of scholars who had devoted their graduate study and subsequent research to literacy and composition theory. For the most part, their perspectives on the introductory curriculum were not practical or one-dimensional responses to understandings of the "problems" in the writing of underprepared students but rather nuanced and deep analyses of multicultural language use, accompanied by new interpretations of student errors. In the words of Rose, as quoted in the introduction to the first year writing outcomes statement, "Error marks the place where education begins."[12]

The language of the above mentioned 1998 guideline for instructors of Introductory English echoes that expressed in the scholarship of the current director who strives to transcend traditional teacher-student relationships in her instructional practice. Rejecting ahistorical, institutionalized conceptions of Freshman English as remedial coursework, Parker advocates introductory instruction in which students begin the process of reflecting critically on language use, both spoken and written. Explicit instruction in reading strategies for close or critical reading is a central component of this first year program. The first-year guidelines contain an unusual degree of insight regarding the educational experiences of urban undergraduates; "Many students enter the university with the tendency to see the texts they read as authoritative and closed. Their past schooling has not encouraged them to cultivate understanding through dialogue between texts and their own experiences and perspectives." Exhibiting an informed understanding of student background in genre and style often absent from descriptions of college level writing programs, the authors provide examples of typical students' background; "For instance, they may not understand the difference between memoirs and academic articles and when it is appropriate to use one or the other or both."

Like her predecessor, Parker's career focused on composition theory and practice. In a book published in the mid-1990s, the then director of Freshmen English explores her understandings of the relationships between various composition theories and instructional practices. This text presents the reader with a director with a strong opposition to introductory coursework that emphasizes either thematic writing or attention to patterns of error. In fact, Parker maintains that a practical emphasis in composition can be misguided. If students receive introductory instruction that fails to develop their analytical capacities, Parker believes that students will suffer from an overdose of skills-based instruction and simply reproduce the status quo through their language use. Influenced by the work of Paulo Freire, this theoretical perspective led her to develop a Freshman English course in which students learned to read and write critically, asking questions about the social purposes of authentic language use. For example, in her writings, Parker describes the work of a student who dissects the meaning of a "human interest" newspaper story about her then six-year-old grandmother's emigration from Ireland to the United States in 1936. Through her analysis of this cutesy piece, the student comes to question the purpose of describing her grandmother as an adorable little "adventurer" when, in reality, she was forced by poverty to travel alone to the United States to live with her aunt. In her paper, this student develops an analysis of the values and purposes served by this type of journalism. According to Parker, this form of composition moves students from simply finding a subject on which to practice skills to true literacy.

According to Bartholomae and other advocates of emancipatory writing, the first year student is an "initiate" in the discourse community of academe.[13] A sample U.S.U. graduate intern syllabus demonstrates this philosophy, complete with directive statements designed to introduce undergraduates to a foreign culture (example: "This course will, if all goes according to plan, teach you the analytical and interpretive skills necessary to be a successful university student."). In "Basic Writing as Cultural Conflict," Tom Fox questions assumptions about both "the initiate" and the nature of the academic discourse community that seem implicit in the language of the Outcomes Statement. He notes that college students, however underprepared they might be, are not beginners when it comes to understanding the specialized language of educational systems, having spent twelve years in schools. Regarding the academic discourse community, he rejects interpretations of this community as static, instead emphasizing that its language should and is modified by new populations and ideas.[14] Therefore, rather than regarding first year college students as beginners, Fox understands them to be at a stage in their development in which they are revisiting old conceptions of both language and school. Fox's challenge to assumptions about college discourse communities is interesting in that it underscores some of the inconsistencies between the language of the first year guidelines and the actual content of some introductory courses, particularly those taught by experienced faculty, such as Deborah Parker. While the statement asserts that freshmen should be viewed as initiates, some freshman assignments, such as the one in which the student in Parker's class reflects on the journalistic interpretation of her grandmother's immigration, create opportunities for interrogation of earlier assumptions about language. In rejecting teacher-centered teaching practice, it seems unlikely that most faculty would embrace a static notion of freshmen as beginners. Perhaps one purpose of references to "initiates" in the outcomes statement is to emphasize that first year students are at the beginning of their college careers, and therefore other departments and faculty must take responsibility for the development of advanced writing proficiency. In this sense, the statement can be viewed as both guidelines for the instruction of Freshman English, and a political statement about the extent to which the freshman program is responsible for undergraduate writing proficiency.

In a 2003 interview, a retired English faculty member recalled that it was his personal selection of the present director and her predecessor as the faculty from whom his somewhat aimless son should take Freshman English that turned his child's life around. Now a graduate student at a prestigious university, this young man pointed to his engagement with Introductory English coursework as the time and place in which he became an intellectual person. The retiree is more than grateful to his former colleagues who, according to him, "run a tight ship."

This interviewee is not sure about the content of the course that was so powerful in his son's life, but one can't help but wonder if this "tight ship" is equally successful for students whose lives are very different from the rebellious son of a college professor. After all, the original interdisciplinary Great Books curriculum was certainly a "tight ship." However, that ship sank not just because it was a victim of history, but also because most faculty lacked a coherent instructional approach to the teaching of classic literature. As mentioned in earlier chapters, those faculty who built compensatory instruction (for example, Campbell's "fluency lessons") into the curriculum were able to teach complex classic texts with success. Since the 1990s, most instructors of the introductory courses are not on their own in the development of instructional methodology. About half the part-time faculty who teach these courses are graduates of the Masters level internship program. Hence, the first year program now has what the founding fathers forgot, professional development that supports the goals of the curriculum.

May Schultz, the director of the Graduate Internship Program in English, is unique. This soft-spoken literacy expert has held several administrative posts at the university, including that of Dean of the School of Education. In her recently published works, one discovers a scholar who draws upon a rich theoretical and practical background as she explains how language and literacy evolve from the cradle to the grave. These texts offer the reader not only the theoretical perspective needed to understand first and second language acquisition, but they also provide models for instructional practice that build upon the language strengths and competencies that underprepared students bring to class. Since the 1980s, experts and practitioners in the field of childhood literacy have drawn upon the work of Freire and other advocates of student-centered discourse communities in the development of meaning-centered early literacy programs. Schultz's background in childhood and adult literacy informs her work with graduate students who, in turn, are able to teach developmentally within a course designed to function as a bridge to college level or advanced literacy. Recently, she has written a text that serves as a handbook for Introductory English instruction. This book functions as a transitional, compensatory experience for graduates of urban high schools. By establishing a framework for an introductory discourse community, Schultz's text both recognizes and compensates for old habits created by overreliance on skills-based instruction, building a ladder to the type of instructional milieu typical of affluent suburban schools. Hence, her course for interns constitutes the type of professional development that is needed for beginning instructors who are in the process of creating student-centered discourse communities. Graduate students engage in a type of instruction that stands in stark contrast to the teacher-centered instructional model practiced by early faculty such as Joyce Campbell who told the original hard-hat crowd, "I'm like the dictionary. Ask me anything."

Schultz's text functions as a foundation for many sections of Introductory English that not only develop traditional reading and writing proficiencies but also create model discourse communities in which students and teachers reflect upon and analyze the nature of language use in multiple contexts, i.e. the students' native communities, as well as the communities of schools and academe. Schultz's book is also the foundation text for the course that she teaches to a selected group of aspiring college teacher interns every spring. In intern Alan Richard's Fall 2002 section of English 101, Schultz's work was the single required text. Because the book contains excerpts from the work of classic writers, as well as lengthy and explicit reading assignments, freshmen enrolled in the courses taught by part-timers who have experienced the graduate internship are introduced to both college-level introductory reading and writing. Initial assignments reflect the thinking of both Parker and Schultz, as students analyze tape-recorded conversations occurring in their discourse communities. Here, Schultz employs techniques common to ethnographic research in the instruction of college level literacy.

A copy of Richard's syllabus for English 101 is an example of a "tight ship." In a 2004 email, he described himself as "quite confident" to teach the introductory course after completing the required "student teaching" seminar which consisted of co-teaching a course with a selected faculty mentor. In addition to this field experience, his graduate coursework provided background and analysis of both canonical texts and recent research in the field of literacy learning. This combination of content, theory, and practice prepared him for his first college class. Given that roughly 50 percent of part-time introductory instructors for the academic year 2003–2004 were current or former graduate interns, this program constitutes a coherent professional development program. The influence of this graduate program extends beyond the walls of U.S.U., as graduates are often hired to teach introductory courses at the local community colleges. Hence, it is sometimes the case that transfer students have received Freshman English instruction that is compatible with that experienced by first-year students at Urban State.

Part and full-time faculty who teach introductory courses also benefit from Schultz and Parker's scholarship in the areas of composition theory and literacy learning. Both women present research to faculty groups and publish articles in journals read by English faculty. Schultz's background in early literacy provides graduate students and faculty with information about whole language learning and other Language Arts innovations of which most Humanities faculty are generally ignorant. Such understanding of K-12 practice facilitates the development of compensatory instruction.

Unlike institutions such as the University of Texas at Austin where faculty and members of the general public crusaded against an introductory program considered to run by a "highly politicized faction of radical literary theorists"[15] or colleges where faculty resent introductory programs viewed as serving English Department interests, there appears to be no one threatening to wrestle control away from those currently in charge of Introductory English. In fact, there is general agreement that the introductory program is strong and coherent, offering appropriate preparation for upper level work. The main problem with the program, according to many faculty and administrators, is that most of the university's graduates do not experience this introductory coursework.

Since the late 1990s, a new course requirement for entering students with less than 30 credits, the first year seminar, also prepares students in the areas of critical reading, writing, thinking, and speaking. Given that many transfer students with 30 credits or less have already completed Freshman English by the time they arrive at Urban State, this innovation serves both to reach those students who might otherwise miss out on preparation for the reading and writing demands of upper-level coursework and retain first-time freshmen who respond positively to the advising and instructional support services that are an aspect of the seminar. The development and design of this new general education requirement are strongly influenced by both the thinking and practice of the directors of Freshmen English and the internship program, as well as long-time English faculty. In an assessment report on the fall 1998 pilot seminars, one finds faculty and student responses that reflect a level of engagement somewhat reminiscent of the early years at this urban campus. Interestingly, many of the features of this innovation, such as small classes with committed full-time faculty were aspects of the original program. Writes one professor in the qualitative comment section, "I had a wonderful group of students, the perfect class size and all in all had fun teaching the course. It was challenging and I tried many new things." Students also responded with an unusual degree of enthusiasm for this course; 85 percent indicated that they would recommend the experience to a friend.[16]

In 2001, the college further addressed the issue of transfer students' preparedness for college-level reading, writing, and study skills. Students transferring up to 89 credits were required to take an intermediate seminar. These courses are taken in fulfillment of a requirement in critical analysis; they consist of, to quote the college catalogue, "an examination of a topic or problem in some depth while addressing such academic capabilities as critical reading, critical thinking, clear writing, academic self-assessment, collaborative learning, information technology, and oral presentation."

Between 1993 and 2003, May Schultz strove to address the problems caused by an excessively wide range of student preparedness through a collaborative that she administered. This organization consisted of regular meetings between representatives of U.S.U.'s Introductory English program and those who instructed similar courses at many of the region's community colleges. The purpose of this venture was the alignment of goals and instructional practice in introductory coursework. Unfortunately, the budget cuts of 2003 eliminated the funds for these meetings. In light of the governor's recently expressed concerns about both retention and graduation rates at state colleges, the termination of this collaboration seems both shortsighted and counterintuitive.

Given that analysis of failure on the writing proficiency reveals that transfer students from community colleges have the most difficulty with this requirement,[17] the elimination of the collaborative may well lead to increases in the number of students who fail to pass this requirement. In addition, the 2002 requirement that students pass this examination before they have earned more than 60 credits, rather than 75 credits, will most likely affect community college transfers in disproportionate numbers. In particular, when one considers that the most common cause of failure is related to reading comprehension, U.S.U.'s introductory coursework's emphasis on explicit reading strategies is both unique and critical to the success of many transfers.

During a recent phone conversation, an administrator involved with the administration of the writing proficiency examination indicated that the introductory programming does provide a good foundation for the development of college level reading and writing. "The problem," she told me, "is that most of the students who take the writing examination did not take our introductory courses." As is the case nationally, the majority of first-time freshmen transfer to other institutions.[18] Hence, well over three-quarters of the students who take the proficiency examination are transfers. For many, this assessment is experienced as disconnected from curriculum. For example, in a recent email, a 2003 graduate told me that she "figured" that she had passed the writing examination, which she took "at the eleventh hour," when she received her diploma. The new requirement that students pass the proficiency before earning more than 60 credits is undoubtedly in response to the number of transfers who fulfill this junior level requirement as they prepare to graduate.

Recent trends in the number of first-time freshmen who enroll at U.S.U. do not indicate any significant change in this population. In 1996, 2,150 students applied for admission to the class of 2000; of the 1,268 who were admitted, 634 enrolled. In 2001, 578 freshmen enrolled.[19]

By the fall of 1996, there were 553 members of the freshman class. Of this group, 55 graduated on or before May 2000, 82 graduated on or before May 2001, and 186 had graduated by May of 2002. Hence, the six-year graduation rate for those entering in 1996 is 35 percent.[20] While the current governor, along with many other politicians and social commentators, employs this graduation rate as an indicator of failure on the part of this urban university, it is important to note that on the national level, in 2003, only 48 percent of those students in the highest income bracket graduated within six years. According to the *Chronicle of Higher Education*, only 7 percent of the lowest-income students graduate within that time period.[21] When considered from this wider context, this urban university is doing a better than average job at graduating low and moderate income first-time freshmen. If the university could increase the number of students who enter as first-time freshmen, then it is logical to assume that the total number of low-income students receiving a bachelor's degree within six years would increase. Given the recent statements by U.S. Senator Joseph Lieberman and others indicating that the low graduation rates of poor students constitute a pressing civil rights issue, one might wish that universities such as U.S.U. could expand enrollments of first-time freshmen to include some of those students who now enroll, often part-time, at community colleges.

CONCLUSION

You can't bring back rigor by assigning rigor.
You can only teach the people who come to class.
EMILY JONES

In 1985, when asked about the merits of recommendations made by Great Books enthusiasts such as William Bennett, Emily Jones said, "If you sit with someone who has read very little and say, 'Now, here's *The Odyssey*,' you may think you're teaching that person some ideas and probably you are teaching some ideas, but to teach that person how to read analytically and question assumptions—No."

Like most of us, Jones was clear about what she understood to be ineffective, weak instruction, and a bit unclear about solutions to chronic, unsolved educational problems at schools such as Urban State. Since the doors to this university opened, faculty have known that most students come to college with a relatively limited level of writing proficiency, study skills, and general knowledge. In the mid-1980s, Jones acknowledged this reality when she stated that because higher education has been democratized, "You can't teach Freshman English the way it was taught twenty or thirty years ago." However, while she did not hand freshmen copies of *The Odyssey*, Jones was involved in the process of compiling readings for the college-wide Proficiency Examination of Writing. To comprehend these selections, readers needed college level general knowledge and reading comprehension.

At that time, students at Urban State typically took the Proficiency before entering their junior year. Therefore, it seems safe to assume that faculty who compiled readings for the exam were operating under the assumption that students were building up a storehouse of general knowledge during their freshmen and sophomore years at college. After all, that was the stated goal of the new Core Curriculum. Yet, both students and faculty often grumbled that undergraduates lacked the background to interpret the readings well enough to write about them in an analytical essay of the type required by the writing proficiency examination. In the mid-1980s, readings focused on topics such as the films of Robert Altman and public health issues; ironically, more recent readings have focused on interpretations of Homer's *Odyssey*.

Since the original general education program was abolished, one of the few things that most parties involved with this urban university can agree on is that introductory curricula at U.S.U. and its "feeder schools" often do not fill the knowledge gaps that underprepared students bring to college. By 1984, transfer students accounted for more than half of the students in the college. The majority of these students came to the University from local community colleges, where many completed their first, if not their second, semester of Introductory English. By the 1990s, two out of three students in the College of Arts and Science were transfer students. In general, high school GPAs and average SAT scores have always been lower for the transfer population than for those students who enter as first time freshmen.[1]

While it is true that you can only teach the students who come to class, just as you can only raise the child you are given, rather than some perfect fantasy child, the limits and potential of either are elastic. As Delpit notes, when we teach students who are not like us, the language used for instruction is often misinterpreted and redefined by students in their own cultural terms.[2] When I took English 101 in 1968, I was "assigned rigor," in the form of the *Old Testament, The Odyssey, Aeneid, The Inferno, Henry IV,* and other canonical texts. Looking back, I'm sure I survived the experience on the strength of my sentence structure alone, as my passing grade had little to do with my ability to appreciate or analyze the classic texts that bored and confused me. To be able to value, interpret, and analyze this sort of literature, I needed Joyce Campbell's "fluency lessons" or some other bridge to understanding that would have permitted me the revelation that classic writers offer perspective on contemporary topics such as sex, violence, love, and revenge. To incorporate the canonical texts into my personal knowledge base, I needed to be able to locate them in a meaningful context. This did not happen, and I responded aimlessly to lackluster writing assignments. The then required four semesters of Introductory English did, however, enable my growth as a literate person, as I later received patient and careful instruction from a professor who responded to my adolescent cliches and quick quips with probing questions and criticism that allowed me to read both classic and contemporary literature for meaning and write and rewrite until I completed a thorough literary analysis. This process gave me so much pleasure and satisfaction that I declared an English major.

In *Lives on the Boundaries*, Mike Rose describes how as a blue-collar undergraduate who wrote grammatically incorrect sentences containing inflated vocabulary, he became engaged in an on-going "conversation" with faculty and students that led eventually to his membership in the community of educated persons. Of the faculty who nourished his interest in the great books, the author says, "What transpired between us was the essence of humane liberal education, and it enabled me to move beyond the cognitive charade of my freshman year."[3]

Rose's story of his life as a learner chronicles the difference that teachers can make when they are able to draw upon the language, values, beliefs, and definitions that students, regardless of background, bring to school. It is the author's high school English teacher, Jack MacFarland, Rose's intellectual and academic savior, who builds a ladder for him to classic literature through role modeling, mentorship, and direct instruction. He does not simply "assign rigor" in the form of classic literature; he involves his students in the excitement of a reader's life. Through it all, MacFarland never, never condescends to the teenage boys; there is no sense of missionary work, only a seat offered at his own personal kitchen table for literate conversation. Rose and his pals find that they are more than starving for the knowledge that expands their relationship with both their remarkable teacher and the literate world he inhabits. Rose's story is very similar to that of Urban State's first dean who recollects vividly the instruction of Mr. Ned Pierce, Yale class of 1914, who taught English at the urban, public commercial high school which he attended as a working-class teenager during the Depression. Although the curriculum was rigid and traditional, Mr. Pierce aroused Millet's early love of history through his careful and intelligent instruction of required reading of the Bible, Dante, and Shakespeare.

The stories of working class adolescents who establish a personal relationship with canonical texts through the influence and instruction of a powerful mentor are moving, but it is unclear how these individual sagas can inform thinking about how to develop meaningful compensatory programs for large populations of underprepared adults and children. We know that Jack MacFarland's counterparts are most often found in elite private schools or affluent suburban high schools, not the underfunded, overcrowded public and parochial schools that most of the hard-hat crowd attend. Even with the extra help and attention provided by his mentor, Mike Rose floundered at Loyola, where he went on scholarship. Again, his English teacher stepped in, providing him with faculty contacts among his friends who could help his favored student play catch-up. In fact, if one simply clocks the hours that this high school teacher dedicated to his favored student's education, it becomes apparent that individualized support is an impossible solution to the general problem of underpreparation.

Dean Millet and the late Professor Sheehan long maintained that the purpose of the original U.S.U. curriculum was to help the hard-hat crowd "catch up" to their more privileged peers. They believed that this was the sort of compensatory education necessary for democracy's survival. In 1965, Stephen Millet and Doug Sheehan believed adamantly that they knew what to do with the students who were about to "come to class." They had a lot more in mind for the children of the urban poor than the isolated memorization of passages of classic works and the names of literary devices and terminology. Motivated by impulses similar to those of Rose's Mr. MacFarland, they designed a curriculum and assembled a faculty that they believed could provide blue-collar college students with access to the cultural knowledge of the highly literate. In their minds, they were waging the academic's war against intellectual improvishment. Their dream was modeled after the theories epoused by men such as Cardinal Newman and Robert Hutchins who envisioned a community of scholars engaged in the pursuit of eternal truths, uncorrupted by education for utility.

Of course, Millet and Sheehan were less than successful in obtaining their goals. For a range of reasons, from the realities of state bureaucracy to the realities of state finances to the realities of history, they were up against nearly impossible odds in their attempt to transmit the traditions and values of Western civilization to the graduates of urban public and parochial schools. By the early 1970s, their curriculum was viewed by many as an instrument of imperialism, and by that decade's end, specialized "education for utility" was almost all there was on most college campuses. As Millet writes in his incomplete, unpublished memoir, "In its sixth year, the common required curriculum was abandoned, a defeat for students to this day. Not that they sense defeat, having no way to measure." He ads cynically, "And not that the country will notice. The idea that a democratic polity may not last without a healthy minority of liberally educated people across all classes rarely surfaces among educators."[4]

By 1988, a year before the first dean left the college that he claimed was "born of the 1960s, broken by the 1970s,"[5] the manual for students who were preparing for the writing proficiency examination reflected little of the spirit and standards that permeated the rhetoric of the founding fathers. All that appeared to remain was a reference to the vaguely expressed idea that the examination assessed skills that were valuable to "citizens of a democracy."

In that same year, at a presentation of the National Academy of Education, Carl Kaestle declared that only two percent of Americans were in a group that can be called "highly literate."[6] According to him, most college graduates fell into a category of functional literates who attained a level of reading and writing proficiency that was devoid of knowledge of both classic works and the traditions and history of Western civilization. Kaestle's statements supported earlier findings by Chall and the National Commission on Excellence (*A Nation at Risk*) in his insistence on a national "literacy crisis." If Kaestle was correct, members of the hard-hat crowd were hardly alone in their ignorance of Homer and Virgil. For by the end of the 1980s, the original Great Books were no longer part of the general knowledge of the young of any social class.

Several scholars present at the 1988 meeting at which Kaestle spoke, voiced concern that the U.S. was in the process of creating a literate ghetto from which the literate community would speak only to academe, rather than the wider national community. Their fears echoed those expressed in a memo written two decades earlier by an Urban State composition theorist who, before computers, cable, and reality TV, worried that Americans were in the process of creating an environment in which "a literate and sophisticated Third World will one day confront an illiterate, visually aided West." Certainly, there was ample evidence that the scope and meaning of the role of education in democracy had narrowed by the close of the twentieth century. At U.S.U., where most undergraduates were now transfer students, the examination of writing proficiency, rather than Freshman English, had become the single experience common to all graduates in the College of Arts and Science. The competencies required for success on this assessment are just one example of a bar set to guarantee a particular skill set, but it is a bar set much lower than that envisioned by either the university's founders, or most champions of public higher education, such as Jefferson, Forester, Reisman, and Rose. For them, a minimum standard of competency in writing is too minimal an educational standard to guarantee an educated citizenry in a democratic society. To this day, the first dean sees such application of minimum standards as mere job training, not higher education.

In the 1980s, I taught sections of English 101 and English 102 that were not particularly dissimilar from the remedial pre-freshman courses that were offered in the early 1970s to underprepared students. Although students were more than satisfied with and interested in my course, I must admit that I used high school level, sometimes even junior high level, reading and writing assignments to develop the proficiencies these undergraduates would need both to pass the examination and to write competently in upper level courses. English 102 was designed around readings connected to a theme of high interest to most students, "Growing Up Below the Medium Income." The course research component consisted of an analysis of a fictional character's chances for success with a real-world intervention. While both locating and assessing the social program required critical thinking and research skills, the assignment was actually a highly structured six-step process, not an independent research project. My previous attempts at traditional research assignments had resulted in a collection of plagiarized papers, odd bits of word sets from related texts, confusing ramblings, and one or two solid papers. On the other hand, my scaffolded assignment did lead to authentic writing and coherence. Somewhat similarly to the City College of New York faculty whom Traub describes, I was too overwhelmed by the remedial needs of many of my students to push the class beyond tenth grade level competencies.

The university to which I returned in the 1980s was a grimy and unusually quiet place. There were few angry editorials in the student paper such as those that once admonished irresponsible peers who ignored their civic duty to attend meetings on campus and national issues. Rushing from class to job to family and friends, students rarely "hung out," sprawled on the grassy slopes that ran toward the sea, as they had in the 1970s. A walk around the campus told a story unto itself. The building in which most of the Introductory English courses were taught was almost as dirty and dull as the Wilson Building that housed the English classes during the 1960s. The only exception to this low-budget institutional image was the glass-cased dean's office. I wondered how students felt as they viewed the immaculate velour upholstery and spotless carpets on their way to their litter strewn, airless classrooms.

By the late 1980s, in the privately managed student cafeteria, there was a sign that read: "No Studying Allowed Here." By 2000, that sign was gone. In the 1980s, the elevators in the administration building ran much better than those that operated in classroom buildings, and the privately managed bookstore did not give students complete refunds on books, even when their section changes were a function of bureaucratic error. While this is not a list of major injustices or even a topic directly relevant to the curriculum of Freshman English, it does paint an unflattering picture of the campus climate, an atmosphere that often felt no friendlier than the Registry of Motor Vehicles. I couldn't help but recall the school's early years when there were no well-furnished administrative offices, no gym, no privately owned bookstore, and the elevators didn't run well for anyone. It is difficult to imagine a "Don't Study Here" sign remaining in the cafeteria for more than five minutes. There were many in administration, on the faculty, and in the student body who would have torn it down. If anything, the 1960s' motto was, "please study here!"

By 2002, the Dean's office was less shiny and new and the classrooms cleaner. No fruitflies hung in the air on a summer afternoon as they had fifteen years earlier. At least the buildings appeared to have experienced a kind of democratization, each room equally solid and plain, and just a bit shabby. Sitting on a decades old threadbare sofa, my window view contained the half-completed multimillion dollar student center. I tried to imagine the type of student who would populate these well-worn rooms and have time to lounge and watch television in the new center. As Kirp asserts in *Shakespeare, Einstein and the Bottom Line*, such costly projects exemplify an era in which "customer" satisfaction often trumps the pursuit of knowledge.[7] It has been almost four decades since the creation of this university in which most resources were delegated to the academic program. Founding faculty and administrators mentioned doing their own typing because there was so little money for support services. The first dean also expressed his aversion to almost all-extracurricular projects, including athletics, if they weakened the academic mission of a school.

By the 1990s, with over two-thirds of the undergraduates in the College of Arts and Sciences entering as transfer students, Urban State had become a sort of degree completion program, a place where the most typical undergraduate was a young adult in her early twenties who had completed the first two years of her undergraduate career at a local community college. This dramatic change in the composition of the student body appears to be mostly a function of the ever escalating cost of tuition beginning with the fiscal crisis of the mid-1970s, the lower per credit cost at community colleges, and clearer articulation agreements between the state universities and many two-year institutions. By the 1990s, many members of the hard-hat crowd believed they could save money by attending a community college for their first 60 credits while receiving provisional acceptance at a state university. The irony is that, given the limited financial aid options available to community college and part-time students, the average U.S.U. student graduates with almost twice the indebtedness of state residents who attend private colleges.[8]

By 2000, first-time freshmen accounted for less than one third of the students in the College of Arts and Sciences. The catalog informs transfer applicants that at least 30 credits out of 120 must be taken at Urban State; hence, all graduates of the college are expected to earn the equivalent of a year's worth of credit before they can earn its degree. Even within these atypically generous parameters, there are exceptions to the 90-credit maximum. The fact that most undergraduates complete only a fraction of their undergraduate education at U.S.U. is especially relevant to issues such as mission and the status of the liberal arts within the undergraduate curriculum. For, while most of the compensatory programs offered at U.S.U. and other public universities (such as CUNY) during the 1970s and early 1980s had a clear commitment to a quality liberal arts education for underprepared students,[9] this is not always the case at community colleges where a vocational orientation is common.[10]

According to Sadovnik, the primary purpose of compensatory higher education is "to compensate for unequal precollege education through remediation, providing a foundation for the successful completion of a college education."[11] The Introductory English program at USU has always had sections that are remedial and often non-credit bearing, but on the whole, this program has rejected the philosophy behind a strictly remedial orientation. From the opening day, the program has emphasized small classes with committed faculty as the best environment in which underprepared students can catch up to their more privileged peers. Today, the orientation of the first year writing program centers on a model of liberating compensatory education that bears little resemblance to ideas about curriculum held by the founding fathers. To a certain extent this change is due to the passage of time and changes in the content of high school curricula nationally, not just in low-income communities. But, it is more than this; the current understanding of "catching up" emphasizes the role of language and literacy, more than comprehension of particular texts or even the learning of particular knowledge. Viewing language and literacy as socially and culturally constructed, the directors have a social-constructivist view of the appropriate curriculum for introductory coursework. Hence, their emphasis on the development of coursework in which students analyze authentic language use.

The guidelines that currently inform the instruction of Introductory English courses led both veteran full- and part-time faculty and graduate student interns to the establishment of discourse communities within the classroom. A 2002–2003 graduate student in English described how he was trained to enter his first section of English 101 through the careful guidance and instruction of the Director of Graduate Internships. Using a book authored by this professor as a common text, the graduate student interns developed their own course within loose guidelines. The former intern described a teacher-training experience not that dissimilar from learning to ride a bike with training wheels. Once he was on his own, he felt quite confident as an instructor. This young man's syllabus mirrors ideas expressed in both the director's text and the First-Year Outcomes Statement. As the first page of his fall 2002 syllabus states, "the course is built around the concept of the discourse community," rather than coverage of particular content. In his section of English 101, tape recorded conversations are often the text that students deconstruct. Other reading and writing assignments come from this text which contains selections from memoirs and ethnographic writings. In her foundational text, the director draws upon recent scholarship in early literacy in directing undergraduates to view writing as a conversation with a community, rather than a solitary experience.

The first-year program is designed so that after completing English 101, students move on to a section of English 102 that is supposed to build upon strengths in analytical reading and writing that are developed in the first semester of freshman composition. In this class, students are expected to read more demanding literary selections and complete a research paper. Unfortunately, according to student accounts, given that the majority of students do not take their first introductory course at U.S.U., much of the instructional time in English 102 is given to skills-building activities that many students describe as "remediation." A college administrator involved with the writing examination supported these student observations with a statement indicating that while English 102 is intended to provide students with the kinds of writing experiences that are evaluated by the writing proficiency, they often complete less demanding assignments. In particular, she mentioned that students often write reports rather than research papers that integrate and synthesize multiple perspectives from multiple sources. Additionally, she noted that since so many students transfer more than 30 credits, the intermediate seminars are the courses in which most students receive writing instruction aimed at preparing students to be competent college-level writers.

As indicated by the administrator mentioned above, the development and delivery of appropriate introductory curricula for underprepared college students presents a major challenge during a period in which over half of our nation's college graduates begin their undergraduate study at an institution that is not the one from which they receive their degrees.[12] Given the attractiveness of inexpensive community colleges, transferring general education credits is even more likely for low-income students.

When there is a mismatch between general education and upper-level coursework, the undergraduate experience is often frustrating and incoherent for students, as well as faculty. Given the current climate of privatization of the cost of public education in which students shop for the least expensive college credits, the practice of transferring credits will only increase. Only colleges that can foster commitment to a four-year learning experience can expect to counter this trend. Only states that subsidize strong and vital public universities and colleges are likely to have the kind of compelling post-secondary programs to which students, especially those of low and moderate income, will make a four-year investment. But, increased levels of appropriations for public higher education are not likely in this state, or most of the nation. There are too many public officials who would agree with Richard Rothstein's 30th Anniversary Essay for the Spencer Foundation in which he maintains that it is a myth that our technologically advanced society will require more highly educated professionals in the future. Instead, he says, "many occupations with middle-class pay—computer and health technicians, equipment repair or finance personnel—demand vocational or on-the-job training, not bachelor's or even associates of arts degrees."[13] In his essay, Rothstein maintains that it is a mistake to encourage "uncritical college ambitions" in 90 percent of high school students when our service economy does not support such aspirations. Such beliefs are not good news for public universities, tied as they are to the needs of local economies. And certainly, such assumptions are not good news for first generation students who aspire to a college education. But, Rothstein's sort of thinking may partly explain why contemporary college and statewide financial aid policies often favor middle and even upper income students over their poorer peers.[14] And, such aid policies may at least partly explain why only 7 percent of college students from the lowest income bracket graduate within six years.[15]

In the introduction to this book, I employed the image of young newlyweds as symbolic of the mission of the new university. Today, if I were pressed to come up with a marital metaphor for this urban university, it would not consist of the original partners, aged but somehow similar. The mission has changed significantly from 1965 when this school was founded "to build a university in the ancient tradition of Western civilization." Then, the founders believed passionately that the future of democracy required expanding the population of the liberally educated to include members of the urban working class. In their efforts to establish an elite-style public university in a state long reluctant to subsidize higher education, they were both bold and naive, but not without political and philosophical allies. At the dawn of the 21st century, conceptualizations of democracy come from ideas learned from television and the Internet, more than the words of Emerson, Thoreau, Jefferson, or Paine, never mind the ancient Greeks.

Today, Urban State University bears more resemblance to a mature couple on their second, third, or even fourth marriage. Although there are important exceptions, the primarily transfer students and mostly graying faculty do not appear to welcome innovations or surprises; they have already taken enough detours. Most students are there to receive a credential, not to change their lives.

As I bring this study to a close, I recall some of the first words I heard as I began research. Years ago, Dean Millet told me that he couldn't stand to look back at the history of this institution. Now, I understand his feeling. This is the story of an institution that evolved from grand ideas about privileged education for the underprivileged to a place where low and moderate-income undergraduates take on significant debt to obtain a piecemeal education that usually takes much more than four years to obtain. I entered U.S.U. in January of 1968 and graduated debt-free in May, 1971. Yes, the taxpayers subsidized my education, including books and even part of my rent. But, the state in which I was born and received a kindergarten through college education also realized a return on this investment in the form of tax dollars and public service. Would I have persisted in my desire to become a college professor if I had left college twenty thousand dollars in debt, completed coursework at three different institutions, and subsequently took six years or more years to graduate? Probably not.

So what, the cynic or "realist" might say? So what if an ordinary kid with mediocre grades from a second-rate public high school doesn't get to be a college professor? So what if thousands like her experience higher education as shopping for the least expensive college credits? If, as Rothstein and others maintain, our new service economy requires fewer graduates in the liberal arts, then the business interests that were invoked as a major reason for this university's creation now seem to deny the need for its existence. The region certainly produces more than enough liberal arts graduates at its private colleges. And, if it doesn't matter if thousands of ordinary low-income high school graduates are denied access to the type of education received by their equally ordinary but more affluent peers, then the issue of the education of underprepared college students is simplified. Like Mike Rose's Mr. MacFarland, we can count ourselves successful when a single exceptional student receives a full scholarship or when one Honors student receives a Rhodes fellowship. The solution to the privatization of public higher education becomes the privatization of our understanding of success.

The promise of a college education for underprepared students is difficult and expensive to realize. In the middle of a conversation about the degree to which this urban university serves its students well, a colleague said, "It's like Brazilian music, there's so much going on." Indeed, there is so much going on, from the above mentioned Honors student who received a Rhodes fellowship to the disgruntled international student who can transfer 90 college credits to this university but finds he is prevented from receiving a coveted American degree by his failure to pass an examination in writing.

We can blame the generally sorry state of the hard-hat crowd's preparedness for college-level work on the public schools, parents, MTV, drugs, video games, the Internet, business interests, school desegregation, racism, poverty, or whatever else we choose. The facts is, as Christopher Jenck's points out in *Inequality*, so much of what happens in any person's life occurs outside of schools; therefore, schools alone can't completely change a person's attitudes or life chances. However, we know very well that schools can teach someone how to write a coherent research paper and learn specific content area knowledge. As mentioned in Chapter 8, research and national reports reveal that by grade four, most low-income students fall behind their more privileged peers in vocabulary development which leads to problems with the reading and writing assignments one generally encounters throughout the rest of the grade four through college continuum. Efforts at designing assignments on which such "concrete learners" can experience success often provide false confidence as underprepared students fall further and further behind their peers in the acquisition of advanced literacy.

As the current design of the first year writing program acknowledges, members of the hard-hat crowd are already part of a culture with particular values and expectations. Maybe it is a culture that values books and ideas, possessions and money, or family and community. I recall a classmate who cherished the memory of his taxi driver father who read quality literature and voted for Adali Stevenson for president twice. Although this student grew up in near poverty and attended poor public schools, his love of literature and the arts cannot simply be attributed to his interaction with the original Great Books curriculum. Likewise, faculty have not necessarily failed when students refuse to get involved in literary analysis or open-ended, creative projects; however, they should figure out how to respond to students who value knowledge for utility over critical thinking. One does not come to college to learn how to make out a job application.

The current trend toward transforming colleges into theme parks in order to attract student consumers moves the mission of higher education further away from the ideals that birthed this public urban university. In addition, the continuation of the arcane reward system of academe further discourages attention to curriculum and instruction for the underprepared. As this study reveals, in general, this is now the terrain of adjuncts and graduate students. Those whose careers are dedicated to the study and delivery of compensatory higher education are generally discouraged by the decline in numbers of low-income college students during the last decade and the persistent achievement gap between these students and their more privileged peers.

This study presents some possible explanations for what many perceive to be the disappointing effect of compensatory programs and curricula in higher education. First, the study reveals that the conditions in which the hard-hat crowd attends college discourage sustained engagement with curricula and learning. Second, even progressive college faculty generally do not develop curriculum or instruction that is informed by research on childhood literacy learning or low-income students' understandings about schools and schooling. In particular, lack of knowledge about students' understandings of "going to school" often guarantees that unreflective and even anti-intellectual in-school attitudes and behaviors will continue in college. Their K-12 experiences not only prepare students for college, they also teach them how to negotiate and interpret educational institutions. Unlike the select group of immigrants who attended CCNY in the first part of the 20th century, most students who attend this urban campus are not well prepared to make the most of college, so a policy of self-reliance often leads to frustration and failure. The professors who taught at CCNY during the 1930s, 1940s, 1950s, and 1960s worked with a group of undergraduates who had attained a high level of literacy before they entered college. Therefore they were able to successfully teach curricula that provided cultural enrichment as well as knowledge in new or advanced subjects. Such a situation no longer exists at City College, and it never existed at Urban State. U.S.U. faculty have always had to teach a student population that includes a significant percentage of functional illiterates who come to college unable to write a coherent paragraph or compare two ideas. Yet, we know that these skills were "covered" in their previous educational experiences, probably beginning in elementary school; what is generally unknown is why students failed to learn. To be successful, instruction in introductory courses must be informed by understanding of the sources of earlier failures.

In the wake of investigations into the events surrounding the national tragedy of September 11, 2001, we have learned that government agencies failed to connect the dots between information separately held. The consequences of this lack of collaboration may have been dire. Somewhat similarly, there are serious consequences from our collective failure to share knowledge between grade levels and disciplines. Since the early 1980s, there has been a great deal of research into literacy learning across the age span; yet, as John Wilson notes in *Higher Education in the Twenty-first Century*, little has changed in the undergraduate curriculum in the last quarter century.[16] One has to wonder why new knowledge about how literacy evolves has failed to affect the nature of college level reading and writing instruction. The first year writing program at U.S.U. is unique in that it is informed by scholarship in the field of literacy learning; but, unfortunately, few graduates complete this two-semester program.

From the Ivies to community colleges, faculty typically share a common complaint: their students are not competent writers. But, complaints may be all academics are willing to share, for in higher education, as in many other organizations, research, ideas, data, and other findings are jealously guarded for future publication, promotion, or prestige. To treat such information as primarily usable or useful to practice often constitutes professional suicide, as well as an invitation to theft by others in need of a good idea. And so, as a community, we generally come up with standards and minimum proficiencies primarily because they exist as phenomena outside of the disciplines; these assessment measures are separate from instruction and learning within the discipline. It is the rare university that ties any measures of accountability to an exit exam from a particular course or course sequence.[17]

Recent developments in New York highlight what the future may hold for public higher education. In November 1999, over strenuous objections from civil liberties groups, alumni, students, faculty, and others, the New York State Board of Regents voted to limit remedial courses to its two-year colleges. A month earlier, the CUNY Board of Trustees, in the face of threats from the mayor, voted to use standardized test scores to determine the requirement of remedial coursework. Hence, passing scores became admissions requirements at four-year institutions; therefore, objections to the removal of university-level compensatory instruction centered on its segregating effect.[18] As noted by Brint and Karabel, low-income students of color are the least likely to transfer from community colleges to four-year institutions.[19]

Given that few dispute that this type of response to underpreparation will lead to segregation by class and race, the academic community must engage the issues that the legislation represents. For the most part, the various forms of compensatory education have not provided a context in which underprepared college students can catch up to their more privileged peers. Every innovation has its individual exceptions to this generalization, but these individual success stories have little effect on trends.

I propose that it is time to connect the dots between research in the fields of schooling in society, literacy learning, composition theory, and general education. The work of Ashton-Warner, Atwell, Brunner, Caulkins, Delpit, Graves, Hawkins, Heath, Rose, Smith, and others explains how environments are created in which children and young adults develop identities as literate people. Without such a sense of self, most children and young adults do not engage in meaningful reading and writing activities outside of school. As Hawkins notes in *The Roots of Literacy*, "adult curiosity flourishes only when in some good measure it has grown from a childhood that has found support for being at home in the world. Neither technical competence nor political judgment can grow, optimally, except from such a base."[20]

The original U.S.U. curriculum failed, at least in part, because the founding fathers did not create an environment in which underprepared students could be "at home." Left to their own invention, some individual faculty members developed strategies that facilitated working class undergraduates' authentic responses to classic texts; Joyce Campbell's "fluency lessons" were clearly designed to create an environment in which students were "freed for wonder and for exploration and enjoyment."[21] Through conversation about contemporary topics, she led undergraduates to an exciting connection with classic works. Forty years ago, New Zealand's Sylvia Ashton-Warner observed that low-income children of color were particularly likely to reject learning in school if they were not "at home" with both school and language learning.[22] Through early literacy instruction centering on organic language use, Ashton-Warner created an environment in which Maori children learned that literature held a connection to their personal perspective on the human condition. The creation of literate discourse communities is not mysterious; if Oprah is able to sell millions of copies of classic texts in Wal-Mart, academe should be able to teach underprepared college students how to read and write for sustained inquiry and learning.

If we can rebuild a foreign nation, why not rebuild a democratic society based on a vibrant system of public education that strives to "teach the people who come to class" with an informed understanding of who they are, how they've been taught, and how they can come to "be at home" with the knowledge base of educated people? Yes, it would be better and more effective to begin this process before grade four. That is just one reason why academics and public school teachers should become "at home" with one another. Yes, college is a difficult place to play catch-up, especially if one has a family and a job. But, as Patricia Cross tells us, goal-oriented adults can learn quickly.[23]

While thinking about how Urban State University and similar institutions can be rebuilt and reinvigorated, it is important to remember that there is an aspect of the original mission that has remained unchanged throughout the years. It is the reason why many insist, contrary to my assessment, that there has always been a consistent mission. At a time when many policies and practices result in lower numbers of students of color attending public universities, it is important to remember that this university remains true to its original impulse to "seek out and support those young people whose race or recent immigration or depressed economic status denies them higher education, and even the expectation of it." Today, the College is more diverse than it was in 1965. However, while acknowledging this commitment to equality, it is important to reflect upon the original commitment to equity that the founding of this university represented.

Sometimes, I think that U.S.U. faculty often approach students and curricula in the same spirit as the mother in Tillie Olsen's now famous story, "I Stand Here Ironing" who wished for her long neglected daughter that she be "more than this dress on the ironing board, helpless before the iron."[24] This is an expression of great caring, coupled with resignation about a past, which although recognized, is not overcome. The mother relies mostly on the wish that her daughter's life will amount to something. As we look toward tomorrow, our challenge appears to be to provide more than wishes and disconnected academic encounters for the students who come to this urban university. Only the future can tell if they will meet Odysseus there.

NOTES

Introduction

1. Levine, Arthur. *Handbook on Undergraduate Curriculum.* (San Francisco: Jossey-Bass Publishers, 1985), 419.
2. Ibid.
3. *Origins*, Yearbook of the Class of 1969, Urban State University, 18.

Chapter 1

1. Brint, Steven, and Karabel, Jerome. *The Diverted Dream: Community Colleges and the Promise of Educational Opportunity*. (New York: Oxford University Press, 1989), 143.
2. Cooper, Frederick M. First Commencement Speech, Urban State University, 1969.
3. Daley, Gerard, interviewed by the author, 7 December 1987.
4. Joe Caulfield Papers, Urban State University Library.
5. Daley, interview.
6. Joe Caulfield Papers, Urban State University Library.
7. Freeland, Richard M. *Academia's Golden Age*. (New York: Oxford University Press, 1992).
8. Walter Hughes to Capital City University Alumni, 4 June 1964, Joe Caulfield Papers, Urban State University Library.
9. Ibid.
10. Admissions data to author from Tom Cefalo, April 1988.
11. Statement of Purpose, Urban State University, 1965.
12. Joe Caulfield Papers, Urban State University Library.
13. Archives, Urban State University Library.
14. Ibid.
15. Daley, interview.
16. Winthrop, Katherine, interviewed by the author, 20 March 1986.

17. Sheehan, Douglas, phone interview by the author, 29 September 1987.
18. Ibid.
19. Sheehan, interview.
20. Ibid.
21. Millet, Stephen, interviewed by author, 2002.
22. Kerr, Clark. *The Uses of the University*. (Cambridge: Harvard University Press, 1995), 36.
23. Lucas, Christopher J. *American Higher Education: A History*. (New York: St. Martin's Press, 1994), 146–153.
24. Ibid., 151.

Chapter 2

1. Millet, Stephen, interviewed by the author, Boston, 6 April 1987.
2. Levine, Arthur. *Handbook on Undergraduate Curriculum*. (San Francisco: Jossey-Bass, 1985), 55.
3. Levine, Arthur, 525.
4. Millet, interview, 1987.
5. Sheehan, Douglas to Susan Merrifield, 2 November 1987, Lesley College, Cambridge, MA.
6. Sheehan, Douglas, phone interview by the author, September 29, 1987.
7. Millet, interview, 1987.
8. Statement of Purpose, Urban State University, 1965.
9. English 101 syllabus, Fall 1965, Joe Caulfield Papers, Urban State University Library.
10. Millet, Stephen, interviewed by the author, 23 July 2002.
11. Millet, Stephen, interview with author, October, 2003.
12. Foerster, Norman. *The American State University*. (Chapel Hill: The University of North Carolina Press, 1937), 18.
13. Foerster, 20.
14. Levine, 359.
15. Foerster, 19.
16. Origins, Yearbook of the Class of 1969, Urban State University, 19.
17. Traub, James. *City on a Hill*. (Reading, MA: Addison-Wesley, 1994).
18. Traub, 66.

Chapter 3

1. Admissions Report (1965–76) The First Six Years, 1 March 1971, Admissions Office, Urban State University, 21.
2. Millet, Stephen, interviewed by the author, Boston, 6 April 1987.
3. Admissions Report (1965–76), 7.
4. Millet, interview, 1987.
5. Millet, interview, 1987.
6. *Origins*, Yearbook of the Class of 1969, Urban State University, 18.

7. Urban State University Catalog, 1970–71, 308.
8. Freedman, Morris. "CCNY Days," *The American Scholar* (Spring 1980).
9. Millet, Stephen, from letter to the editor of an alternative newspaper, 10 May 1979.
10. Traub, James. *City on a Hill.* (New York: Addison-Wesley, 1994), 9.
11. Ibid.
12. "Sixty Minutes," CBS News, April 20, 1975.
13. Ibid.
14. Secondary School College Admissions Data (1965–76).
15. Sadovnik, Alan. *Equity and Excellence in Higher Education.* (New York: Peter Lang Publishing, Inc., 1994), 30.
16. Sadovnik, 1.
17. Joplin, Zack, interview by the author, 22 April 1987.
18. Fields, David, interview by the author, 8 October 1987
19. Fields, interview.
20. Curtis, Elizabeth, interview by the author, 29 October 1987.
21. Clarke, Will, interview by the author, 3 June 1987.
22. Joplin, Zack, interview by author, 20 June 2003.
23. Admissions Data, Office of Admissions, Urban State University.
24. Curtis, interview.
25. Ryan, Alvan. "Liberal Education: Its Purpose and Significance," *Hebron Academy Alumni Bulletin* (Spring 1959), 16–20.
26. O'Malley, Ian, Freshman Committee Chairman, Memo to English Department, April, 1966.
27. Fields, interview.
28. Ibid.
29. Cooper, Bob, interview by the author, 26 May 1987.
30. Cormack, Laura, interview by the author, 18 March 1988.
31. Memorandum, Noel Bliss to the English Department re: Freshman Committee, 1969, Joe Caulfield Papers, Urban State University Library.
32. Millet and Sheehan interviews.
33. Foerster, Norman. *The American State University.* (Chapel Hill: The University of North Carolina Press, 1937), 262–263.
34. Campbell, Joyce, interview by the author, 5 November 1987.
35. Campbell, interview.
36. Ibid.
37. Collected interviews.
38. Fields, interview.
39. Campbell, interview.
40. Adams, Jude, interview by the author, 6 October 1987.
41. Campbell, interview.
42. Ibid.
43. Goswami, Dixie, and Peter Stillman, ed. *Reclaiming the Classroom.* (Upper Montclair: Boynton/Cook Publishers, 1987), 76.
44. Ibid., 77.
45. Sheehan, Douglas, phone interview.
46. Curtis, interview.
47. Cooper, interview.

48. English 101 class assignment, 1967, Author's collection, Lesley College, Cambridge, MA.
49. Admissions Report (1965–76), 22.
50. Anonymous faculty gradebooks.
51. Cefalo, Thomas, interview by the author, 16 March 1988.
52. Wakefield, Dan, author acknowledges, source unknown, 1967.
53. Roberts, Ann, interview by the author, 28 October 1987.
54. Roberts, interview.
55. Roberts, interview.
56. Ibid.
57. Memorandum, Freshman Committee, November 19, 1969, Joe Caulfield Papers, Urban State University Archives.
58. Schneider, Margaret, Memo to the English Department, December 8, 1969, Joe Caulfield Papers, Urban State University Archives.
59. Ibid.
60. Ibid.
61. Ibid.
62. Schneider, Margaret, interview by the author, 15 January 1988.
63. Sadovnik, 31.

Chapter 4

1. Bloom, Harold. *The Closing of the American Mind.* (New York: Simon and Schuster, 1987), 313.
2. Daley, Gerard, interview by the author, 7 December 1987.
3. Galvin, Albert, lecture presented to graduate students in 1987.
4. Letters to the editor, 10 May 1979.
5. Memorandum, Margaret Schneider to English Department, 10 December 1969, Joe Caulfield Papers, U.S.U. Archives.
6. English Department Memo, November 29, 1969, Joe Caulfield Papers, U.S.U. Archives.
7. Curtis, Elizabeth, interview by the author, 29 October 1987.
8. Curtis, interview.
9. Admissions Report (1965–76) The First Six Years, 1 March 1971, Admissions Office, Urban State University, 21.
10. Minutes of University Senate, 1970–71, Joe Caulfield Papers, U.S.U. Archives.
11. Ibid.
12. Cefalo, Thomas, interview by the author, 16 March 1988.
13. Elizabeth Curtis to English Department, 1970, Joe Caulfield Papers, U.S.U. Archives.
14. Ibid.
15. English Department to University Senate, 10 April 1970, Joe Caulfield Papers Papers, U.S.U. Archives.
16. Campbell, Joyce, Alan Paine, and David Fields, interviewed by the author, 1 October–5 November 1987.
17. Frank, Judith, interviewed by author, July, 2002.

18. English 112 class assignment, Spring 1971, Author's collection, Lesley College, Cambridge, MA.
19. Adler-Kassner, Linda. "The Shape of the Form: Working Class Students and the Academic Essay," in *Teaching Working Class*, edited by Sherry Lee Linkon. (Boston: University of Massachusetts Press, 1999), 90.
20. Hamilton, Bruce, interview by the author, 27 March 1986.
21. Minutes of the University Senate, 11 March 1971, Joe Caulfield Papers, Urban State University Archives.
22. Levine, Arthur. *Handbook on Undergraduate Curriculum.* (San Francisco: Jossey-Bass, 1985), 371.
23. Minutes of the University Senate, 11 March 1971.
24. Hamilton, interview.
25. Levine, 390–394.
26. Minutes of the University Senate, 25 March 1971, Joe Caulfield Papers, U.S.U. Archives.
27. Winthrop, Katherine, interviewed by the author, 25 March 1986.
28. Levine, 393.

Chapter 5

1. Millet, Stephen, interviewed by the author, 6 April 1987.
2. Galvin, Albert, lecture at Ivy League School of Education, 1987.
3. Brint, Steven, and Jerome Karabel. *The Diverted Dream: Community Colleges and the Promise of Educational Opportunity in America, 1900–1985*. (New York: Oxford University Press, 1989), 113–115.
4. Paine, Alan, interview by the author, Medford, MA, 1 October 1987.
5. Campbell, Joyce, interview by the author, 5 November 1987.
6. Millet, John D. *Conflict in Higher Education* (San Francisco: Jossey-Bass, 1984), 46.
7. Memorandum, Freshman English Sub-Committee to English Department, 8 February 1970, Joe Caulfield Papers, U.S.U. archives.
8. Ibid.
9. Ohmann, Richard. *English in America: A Radical View of the Profession.* (New York: Oxford University Press, 1976), 141.
10. Joplin, Zack, interview by the author, July 2003.
11. Fields, David, interview by the author, 8 October 1987.
12. Memorandum, Wilfred Skye to English Department, 21 March 1972, Joe Caulfield Papers, U.S.U. Archives.
13. Cooper, Bob, interview by the author, 26 May 1987.
14. Fields, David, interview.
15. Ibid.
16. Ibid.
17. Lucas, Christopher J. *American Higher Education: A History.* (New York: St. Martin's Press, 1994), 291.
18. Curtis, Elizabeth, interview by the author, 29 October 1987.
19. Gross, Theodore L. "Chairman's Report," *The City College Newsletter*, January, 1972.

20. Ibid.
21. Cormack, Laura, interview by the author, 18 March 1988.
22. Memorandum, Chester Hunt to English Department, 10 April 1972, Joe Caulfiled Papers, U.S.U. archives.
23. Enrollment data, Office of Institutional Research and Planning, Urban State University.
24. Curtis, interview.
25. Cormack, interview.
26. Liz Vermeer and Alan Paine to freshman staff, August 23, 1972, Joe Caulfield Papers, U.S.U. archives.
27. College Admissions Data (1965–76), Admissions Office, Urban State University.
28. Author's recollections of teaching in summer program.
29. DeGaule, email.
30. Paine, interview.
31. Ibid.
32. Connolly, Paul, and Teresa Vilardi. *New Methods in College Writing Programs.* (New York: The Modern Language Association of America, 1986), 106.
33. Joplin, Zack, interview by the author, 22 April 1987.
34. Bob Cooper to Freshman Staff, 1975, Joe Caulfield Papers, U.S.U. archives.
35. Paine, interview.
36. Ibid.
37. William Evans and Bob Cooper to English 101 Staff and Student Teachers, February 14, 1972, Joe Caulfield Papers, U.S.U. archives.
38. Paine, interview.
39. Ibid.
40. Ibid.
41. Whipple, William R., "Collaborative Learning: Recognizing It When We See It," *AAHE Bulletin*, Oct. 1987:3.
42. Paine, interview.
43. Paine, Alan, "Making Open Admission Work: The Uses of Popular Writing in the Classroom," lecture presented at 1974 Conference on College Composition and Communication, April 4–6, 1974.
44. Ibid.
45. Ibid.
46. Cross, Patricia K. *Adults as Learners.* (San Francisco: Jossey-Bass, 1981), 189.
47. Paine, interview.
48. Wilfred Skye to freshman staff, 1973, Joe Caulfield Papers, U.S.U. archives.
49. Cormack, interview.
50. Paine, interview.
51. Paine, interview.

Chapter 6

1. Cooper, Bob, interview by the author, 26 May 1987.
2. Brint, Steven, and Karabel, Jerome. *The Diverted Dream: Community Colleges and the Promise of Educational Opportunity in America: 1900–1985.* (New York: Oxford University Press, 1989), 115–117.

3. Newsweek, "Why Johnny Can't Write." 8 Dec. 1975, 58.
4. Brint and Karabel, 186–188.
5. Ibid.
6. U.S.U. student paper from September 25, 1973, U.S.U. Archives.
7. Ibid.
8. Cooper, interview.
9. Ibid.
10. Memorandum, Phil Soule to Executive Committee of English Department, April 8, 1974, Joe Caulfield Papers, U.S.U. Archives.
11. Cooper, interview.
12. Cooper, Bob. "A Basic Definition of Freshman Courses That Give Credit for Training in Writing," 1974, Joe Caulfield Papers, U.S.U. Archives.
13. Cooper, Bob. "Draft of a proposal for a new and preliminary term of Freshman English," 1975, Joe Caulfield Papers, U.S.U. Archives.
14. Memorandum, Bob Cooper to English Department, "Report on the Evaluation of Eng. 101 and Eng. 110 sections given last year," 2 April 1975, Joe Caulfield Papers, U.S.U. Archives.
15. Cooper, interview.
16. Cormack, Laura, interview by the author, 18 March 1988.
17. Ibid.
18. Cooper, interview.
19. Ibid.
20. Ibid.
21. Ibid.
22. Memorandum to English Department, 1976, Joe Caulfield Papers, U.S.U. Archives.
23. *Getting to the Core: A Report to the Ford Foundation*, 1978.
24. Cooper, interview.
25. Soule, Phil, interview by the author, 10 November 1987.
26. Soule, interview.
27. Stein, Jake, interview by author, 9 July 2003.
28. Soule, interview.
29. Ibid.
30. Ibid.
31. Ibid.
32. Memorandum, Phillip Soule to the English Department, 1976, Joe Caulfield Papers, U.S.U. Archives.
33. Personnel Planning Document (1976–77), English Department, Joe Caulfield Papers, U.S.U. Archives.
34. Memorandum, Art Hull to English Department, "Of Vast Importance," 1976, Joe Caulfield Papers, U.S.U. Archives.
35. Hart, interview.
36. Ibid.
37. Ibid.
38. Ibid.
39. Ibid.
40. Soule, Phil. Memo to the English Department, 1977, Joe Caulfield Papers, U.S.U. Archives.
41. Ibid.

Chapter 7

1. *Getting to the Core: A Report to the Ford Foundation*, 1978, 2.
2. 1983–85 Urban State University Catalogue 44.
3. Levine, Arthur, *Handbook on Undergraduate Curriculum* (San Francisco: Jossey-Bass, 1985), 393.
4. Minutes of Faculty Senate, 1977, Joe Caulfield Papers, U.S.U. Archives.
5. Ibid.
6. Connolly, Paul, and Teresa Vilardi. *New Methods in College Writing Programs: Theories in Practice.* (New York: Modern Language Association, 1986), 96.
7. Connolly and Vilardi, 33.
8. Connolly and Vilardi, 107.
9. Urban State University Catalogue, 1978.
10. Nine Elements of Proficiency in Writing: A Manual for Students in CAS, U.S.U. Fundamental Skills Committee, 1977.
11. U.S.U. Website listing of peer institutions, 2003.
12. Ohmann, Richard. *English in America.* (New York: Oxford University Press, 1976), 94.
13. Phillip Soule's Voluntary Exit Exam for Eng. 102, 1976, Joe Caulfield Papers, U.S.U. archives.
14. Fields, Leigh, interview by the author, Boston, 2 February 1988.
15. Nine Elements of Proficiency in Writing: A Manual for Students in CAS, U.S.U. Fundamental Skills Committee, 1977, 5.
16. Cooper, Bob, interview by the author, 26 May 1987.
17. Levine, 231.
18. Ibid.
19. Ibid.
20. Lucas, Christopher J. *American Higher Education: A History.* (New York: St. Martin's Press, 1994), 291.
21. Hamilton, Bruce, interview by the author, Boston, 11 April 1988.
22. Hamilton, interview.
23. Ibid.
24. Ibid.
25. First Year Writing Outcomes Statement, English Department, U.S.U., 1998.

Chapter 8

1. Campbell, Joyce, interview by the author, 5 November 1987.
2. Anonymous faculty interviews.
3. Fields, David, interview by the author, 8 October 1987.
4. Fields, interview.
5. Franklin, Mark, interview by the author, 7 November 1985.
6. Jones, Emily, interview by the author, 29 October 1985.
7. Jones, interview.
8. Ibid.
9. Swanson, Joy, interview by the author, 3 December 1987.

10. Campbell, interview.
11. Jones, interview.
12. Ibid.
13. Ibid.
14. Statement made by Jones during Fall '83 meeting of Freshman Writing Staff.
15. "Description of English 101–102," Urban State University College of Arts and Sciences, archives.
16. Jones, interview.
17. Ibid.
18. Ibid.
19. Memorandum, Bob Cooper, Henry Thompson, and Emily Jones to All Faculty, October 1985, author's collection, Lesley College, Cambridge, MA.
20. Ibid.
21. Ibid.
22. Collected faculty interviews.
23. Cooper, interview.
24. Statements made during Fall '83 meeting of Freshman Writing Staff.
25. Fields, interview.
26. Cooper, interview.
27. Piken, Nora, interviewed by the author, September 2002.
28. Gormley, Matthew, interview by the author, 21 October 2002.
29. Bell, Lee, phone conversation with Office of Institutional Research, 10 July 2003.
30. Stein, 10 July 2003
31. Holton, Gerald, "An Insider's View of 'A Nation at Risk' and Why It Still Matters," *The Chronicle Review*, 25 (April 2003), B13.
32. Chall, Jeanne. "Literacy: Trends and Explanations," *Educational Researcher*, 12 (Nov. 1983), 3–8.
33. Chall, Jeanne S., Vicki A. Jacobs, and Luke E. Baldwin. *The Reading Crisis: Why Poor Children Fall Behind.* (Cambridge: Harvard University Press, 1990), 28–34.
34. Soule, Phillip, interview by the author, 10 November 1987.
35. Jones, interview.
36. Ibid.
37. Merrifield, Susan. "When Failure Is Discrimination," in *When Children Don't Learn*, ed. Barry Franklin. (New York: Teachers College Press, 1998), 126.
38. Belanoff, Pat. "Language: Closings and Openings," in *Working Class Women in the Academy*, ed. Michelle Tokarezyk and Elizabeth Fay. (Amherst: University of Massachusetts Press, 1993), 253.
39. Barnes, Ella, interview by author, 29 August 2002.

Chapter 9

1. Millet, John D. *Conflict in Higher Education: State Government Coordination Versus Institutional Indepence.* (San Francisco: Jossey-Bass, 1984), 196.
2. Arone, Michel. "State Spending on College Drops for the First Time in 11 Years" in *The Chronicle of Higher Education*, 16 January 2004, A25.
3. Wilson, John. "The Canon and the Curriculum" in *American Higher Education in*

the Twenty-first Century, ed. Phillip G. Altbach, Robert O. Berdahl, and Patricia J. Gumport. (Baltimore: The John Hopkins University Press, 1999), 427.

4. Synthesis of information contained in Parker's publications, presentations, and conversations.
5. National Alliance of Business, 21st Century Workforce Commission (Washington, DC, 2000), 13.
6. Freire, Paulo, and Antonio Faundez. *Learning to Question.* (New York: Continuum, 1989).
7. Risher, Howard. "Behind the Big Picture: Employment Trends in the 1990's," *Compensation and Benefits Review* 29, no. 1 (Jan.-Feb. 1997): 8.
8. Brint, Steven, and Jerome Karabel. *The Diverted Dream: Community Colleges and the Promise of Educational Opportunity in America*, 1900–1985. (New York: Oxford University Press, 1989), 187.
9. Longo, Ernest. *Introduction to Urban State University Planning Report*, March 14, 1990.
10. Office of Institutional Research, phone conversation with Lee Bell, July 2003.
11. Lavin, David E. "Policy Change and Access to 2- and 4-Year Colleges," *American Behavioral Scientist*, 43 No. 7 (April 2000), 1140.
12. Rose, Mike. *Lives on the Boundaries.* (New York: Simon & Schuster, 1999).
13. Bartholomae, David. "When a Writer Can't Write," in *Inventing the University*, ed. Mike Rose. (Englewood Cliffs, NJ: Guilford Press, 1985), 134–165.
14. Fox, Tom. "Basic Writing as Cultural Conflict" in *Critical Literacy in Action*, ed. Ira Shor and Caroline Pari. (Portsmouth, NH: Heinemann, 1999), 68–86.
15. Wilson, John in Altach, Berdahl, and Gumport, 434–435.
16. *Assessment Report on the First-Year Seminar Program Pilot Course*, Urban State University, 8 April 1999.
17. Phone conversation with U.S.U. administrator, December, 2003
18. Shoenberg et al. *General Education in an Age of Student Mobility.* (Washington, DC: Association of American Colleges and Universities, 2001), 19–25.
19. U.S.U. institutional research, 8 January 2003.
20. Ibid., 1 December 2003.
21. Burd, Stephen. "Liberman Calls for More Accountability from Colleges" in *Chronicle of Higher Education*, April 26, 2002, A25.

Conclusion

1. Institutional research, Urban State University Website.
2. Delpit, Lisa. "The Silenced Dialogue: Power and Pedagogy in Educating Other People's Children," *The Harvard Educational Review*, Vol.58, 1988, 280–298.
3. Rose, Mike. *Lives on the Boundary: The Struggles and Achievements of America's Underprepared.* (New York: The Free Press, 1989), 48.
4. Millet, Stephen, part of unpublished memoir presented to the author in October, 2003.
5. Ibid.
6. Kaestle, Carl, "The Acquisition of High Literacy," Lecture at Harvard School of Education, Cambridge, MA, 13 May 1988.

7. Kirp, David L. *Shakespeare, Einstein, and the Bottom Line*. (Cambridge: Harvard University Press, 2003).
8. Yahoo! College Facts & Figures from Thomson & Peterson's, 21 August 2003.
9. Sadovnik, Alan R. *Equity and Excellence in Higher Education: The Decline of a Liberal Education Reform*. (New York: Peter Lang Publishing, Inc., 1994), 2.
10. Brint, Steven, and Jerome Karabel. *The Diverted Dream: Community Colleges and the Promise of Educational Opportunity in America, 1900–1985*. (New York: Oxford University Press, 1989), 161–163.
11. Sadovnik, 1.
12. Shoenberg, Robert, et al. *General Education in an Age of Student Mobility*. (Washington, DC: Association of American Colleges and Universities, 2001), 3.
13. Rothstein, Richard. *"Out of Balance: Our Understanding of How Schools Affect Society and How Society Affects Schools."* (Chicago: The Spencer Foundation, 2002), 7.
14. Kirp, 16–25.
15. Burd, Stephen. "Lieberman Calls for More Accountability from Colleges" in *The Chronicle of Higher Education*, April 26, 2002, A25.
16. John K. Wilson. "The Canon and the Curriculum: Multicultural revolution and Traditionalist Revolt" in Altbach, Berdahl, and Gumport's *American Higher Education in the Twenty-first Century: Social, Political, and Economic Challenges*, 427–430.
17. Connolly, Paul, and Teresa Vilardi. *New Methods in College Writing Programs: Theories in Practice*. (New York: The Modern Language Association, 1986).
18. Selected New York newspaper articles, 1998–2000.
19. Brint and Karabel, 205–232.
20. Hawkins, David. *The Roots of Literacy*. (Boulder: University of Colorado Press, 2000), 2.
21. Hawkins, 2.
22. Ashton-Warner. *Teacher*. (New York: Simon & Schuster, 1963).
23. Cross, Patricia. *Adults as Learners*. (SanFrancisco: Jossey-Bass Publishers, 1981), 88–90.
24. Olsen, Tillie, "I Stand Here Ironing," *Tell Me A Riddle*. (New York: Dell, 1961), 9–21.

BIBLIOGRAPHY

Altbach, P. G., R. O. Berdahl, and P. J. Gumport. *American Higher Education in the Twenty-first Century*. Baltimore: The Johns Hopkins University Press, 1999.

Altbach, P. G., and R. O. Berdahl., eds. *Higher Education in American Society*. Buffalo: Prometheus Books, 1981.

Anthony, Robert N., and David W. Young. *Management and Control in Nonprofit Organizations*. Homewood, IL.: Richard D. Irwin, Inc., 1984.

Apple, Michael W. *Ideology and Curriculum*. Boston: Routledge & Kegan Paul, 1979.

Applebee, Arthur N. *Tradition and Reform in the Teaching of English: A History*. Urbana: National Council of Teachers of English, 1974.

Association of American Colleges. *Integrity in the College Curriculum: A Report to the Academic Community*. Washington, DC: AAC, 1985.

Association of American Colleges and Universities. *General Education in an Age of Student Mobility*. Washington, DC: AAC&U, 2001.

Ashton-Warner, Sylvia. *Teacher*. New York: Simon and Schuster, 1963.

Astin, A. C. *The American Freshman: National Norms for Fall 1986*. Los Angeles: University of California, Higher Education Research Institute, 1986.

Baldridge, J. V., and T. E. Deal. *Managing Change in Educational Organizations*. Berkeley: McCutchan, 1975.

Banks, J. A. *Multicultual Education: Theory and Practice*. Boston: Allyn and Bacon, 1988.

Beecher, Tony, and Stuart Maclure. *The Politics of Curriculum Change*. London: Hutchinson & Co., 1978.

Bennett, William J. *To Reclaim a Legacy: A Report on the Humanities in Higher Education*. Washington, DC: National Endowment for the Humanities, 1984.

Bloom, Allan. *The Closing of the American Mind*. New York: Simon and Schuster, 1987.

Bloom, Lynn Z., Donald A. Daiker, and Edward M. White, ed. *Composition in the Twenty-first Century: Crisis and Change*. Carbondale: Southern Illinois University Press, 1996.

Boyer, Ernest L. *College*. New York: Harper and Row, 1987.

Brint, Steven, and Jerome Karabel. *The Diverted Dream: Community Colleges* and *the Promise of Educational Opportunity*, 1900–1985. New York: Oxford University Press, 1989.

Britton, James, Burgess, T., Martin, N., McLeod, A., and Rosen, H. *The Development of Writing Abilities*. Urbana: National Council of Teachers of English, 1977.

Bruffee, Kenneth A. *A Short Course in Writing*. Cambridge: Winthrop Publishers, Inc., 1972.

Burhans, Clinton S., Jr. "The Teaching of Writing and the Knowledge Gap." *College English*, 45 (1983): 639–656.

Carnegie Council on Policy Studies in Higher Education. *Changing Practices in Undergraduate Education*. Berkeley: Carnegie Foundation for the Advancement of Teaching, 1976.

Carnegie Council on Policy Studies in Higher Education. *The Federal Role in Postsecondary Education: Unfinished Business*, 1975–80. San Francisco: Jossey-Bass, 1975.

Carnegie Foundation for the Advancement of Teaching. *Missions of the College Curriculum*. Washington: Jossey-Bass, 1977.

Carnochan, W. B. *The Battleground of the Curriculum*. Stanford: Stanford University Press, 1993.

Cavitch, David, ed. *Life Studies: A Thematic Reader*. New York: St. Martin's Press, 1983.

Chall, Jeanne S. "Literacy Trends and Explanations." *Educational Researcher*. Nov. 1983.

Chall, Jeanne S., Vicki A. Jacobs, and Luke E. Baldwin. *The Reading Crisis: Why Poor Children Fall Behind*. Cambridge: Harvard University Press, 1990.

Chickering, Arthur W., et al. *Developing the College Curriculum: A Handbook for Faculty & Administrators*. Washington: Council for the Advancement of Small Colleges, 1977.

College Entrance Examination Board. *Academic Preparation for College: What Students Need to Know and Be Able to Do*. New York, 1983.

Conant, James B. *Shaping Educational Policy*. New York: McGraw-Hill Book Co., 1964.

Connolly, Paul, and Teresa Vilardi. *New Methods in College Writing Programs: Theories in Practice*. New York: The Modern Language Association of America, 1986.

Cross, Patricia K. *Accent on Learning: Improving Instruction and Reshaping the Curriculum*. Washington: Jossey-Bass, 1976.

Cross, Patricia K. *Adults as Learners*. Washington: Jossey-Bass, 1981.

Cross, Patricia K. *Beyond the Open Door: New Students to Higher Education*. Washington: Jossey-Bass, 1971.

Delpit, Lisa D. "Skills and Other Dilemmas of a Progressive Black Educator." *Harvard Educational Review*, 56, No. 4.

Delpit, Lisa D. "The Silenced Dialogue: Power and Pedagogy in Educating Other People's Children." *Harvard Educational Review*, 58, No.3, August 1988.

Diamond, Robert M. Designing and *Assessing Courses and Curricula: A Practical Guide*. San Francisco: Jossey-Bass, 1998.

Education Commission on the States. *A Summary of Major Reports on Education*. Denver: 1983.

Flower, Linda, and J. R. Hayes. "A Cognitive Process Theory of Writing." *College Composition and Communication*, Vol. 32, 1981.

Flower, Linda. *Problem-Solving Strategies for Writing*. New York: Harcourt Brace Jovanovich, Inc., 1981.

Foerster, Norman. *The American State University*. Chapel Hill: The University of North Carolina Press, 1937.

Franklin, Barry M. ed. *When Children Don't Learn: Student Failure and the Culture of Teaching*. New York: Teachers College Press, 1998.
Freedman, Morris. "CCNY Days." *The American Scholar*, Spring 1980.
Freeland, Richard M. *Academia's Golden Age*. New York: Oxford University Press, 1992.
Freire, Paulo, and Donaldo Macedo. *Literacy: Reading the Word and the World*. South Hadley, MA: Bergin & Garvey, 1987.
Gamson, Zelda F. *Liberating Education*. San Francisco: Jossey-Bass, 1984.
Gibson, Walker. *A Style Study for Readers and Writers*. New York: Random House, 1969.
Giroux, Henry. *Schooling and the Struggle for Public Life: Critical Pedagogy in the Modern Age*. Minneapolis: University of Minnesota Press, 1988.
Goleman, Judith. *Working Theory: Critical Composition Studies for Students and Teachers*. Westport: Bergin & Garvey, 1995.
Gordon, Raymond L. *Interviewing: Strategy, Techniques, and Tactics*. Homewood, IL: Dorsey Press, 1980.
Goswami, Dixie, and Peter Stillman, ed. *Reclaiming the Classroom*. Upper Montclair: Boynton/Cook Publishers, 1987.
Grant, G., and David Riesman. *The Perpetual Dream: Reform and Experiment in the American College*. Chicago: University of Chicago Press, 1978.
Griffin, Williams, ed. *Teaching Writing in All Disciplines*. Washington: Jossey-Bass, 1982.
Hall, James W., ed. *In Opposition to Core Curriculum*. Westport, CT: Greenwood Press, 1982.
Havighurst, Robert J. *American Higher Education in the 1960's*. Columbus: Ohio State Press, 1960.
Hawkins, David. *The Roots of Literacy*. Boulder: University of Colorado Press, 2000.
Heath, Shirley B. *Ways with Words*. Cambridge: Cambridge University Press, 1983.
Hirsh, E. D., Jr. *Cultural Literacy: What Every American Should Know*. Boston: Houghton Mifflin Company, 1987.
Hodgkinson, Harold L. *Institution in Transition*. New York: McGraw-Hill, 1971.
Holdaway, D. *The Foundations of Literacy*. New York: Scholastic, 1979.
Holleb, Doris B. *Colleges and the Urban Poor*. Lexington, MA: D. C. Heath, 1972.
Howe, H. H., II. *Symposium on the Year of the Reports: Responses from the Education Community*. Cambridge: Harvard Ed. Review, 1984.
Jencks, Christopher, and David Riesman. *The Academic Revolution*. New York: Doubleday & Co., Inc., 1968.
Jencks, Christopher, Smith, M., Acland, H., Bane, M., Cohen, D., Gintis, H., Heyns, B., and Michelson, S. *Inequality: A Reassessment of the Effect of Family and Schooling in America*. New York: Basic Books, 1972.
Kaestle, Carl F. et al. *Literacy in the United States: Readers and Reading Since 1880*. New Haven: Yale University Press, 1991.
Kerr, Clark. *The Uses of the University*. Cambridge: Harvard University Press, 1995.
Kirp, David L. *Shakespeare, Einstein, and the Bottom Line: The Marketing of Higher Education*. Cambridge: Harvard University Press, 2003.

Kirsch, I., and A. Jungeblut. *Literacy: Profiles of America's Young Adults*. Wasington, DC: National Assessment of Educational Progress, 1986.

Kitzhaber, Albert R. *Themes, Theories, and Therapy: The Teaching of Writing in College*. New York: McGraw-Hill, 1963.

Kozol, Jonathan. *Illiterate America*. New York: Doubleday, 1985.

Kozol, Jonathan. *Savage Inequalities*. New York: Crown Publishers, Inc., 1991.

Kutz, Eleanor. *Exploring Literacy: Reading, Writing, and Research about Discourse Communities*. Boston: Addison Wesley Longman, 2004.

Kutz, Eleanor. *Language and Literacy: Studying Discourse in Communities and Classrooms*. Portsmouth, NH: Boynton/Cook Publishers, 1997.

Kutz, Eleanor, Suzy Q. Groden, and Vivian Zamel. *The Discovery of Competence*. Portsmouth, NH: Heinemann, 1993.

Kutz, Eleanor, and Hephzibah Roskelly. *An Unquiet Pedagogy: Transforming Practice in the English Classroom*. Portsmouth, NH: Heinemann, 1991.

Lazerson, Marvin, et al. *An Education of Value*. New York: Cambridge University Press, 1985.

Levine, Arthur. *Handbook on Undergraduate Curriculum*. San Francisco: Jossey-Bass, 1985.

Levine, Arthur. *Why Innovation Fails: The Institutionalization and Termination of Innovation in Higher Education*. Albany: State University of New York Press, 1980.

Loban, William. *Language Development: Kindergarten through Grade 12*. Urbana, IL: National Council of Teachers of English, 1976.

Lucas, Christopher J. *American Higher Education: A History*. New York: St. Martin's Press, 1994.

MacDonald, Barry, and Rob Walker. *Changing the Curriculum*. London: Open Books, 1976.

The Massachusetts Review. *Issue on the Urban University*. Amherst: The Massachusetts Review, VIII (1967), No. 3.

Millet, John D. *Conflict in Higher Education*. San Francisco: Jossey-Bass, 1984.

National Commission on Excellence in Education. *A Nation at Risk*. Washington, DC: Department of Education, 1983.

National Institute of Education. *Involvement in Learning: Realizing the Potential of American Higher Education*. Washington: 1984.

Ohman, Richard. *English in America*. New York: Oxford University Press, 1976.

Olsen, Tillie. *Tell Me a Riddle*. New York: Dell. 1961.

Ravitch, Diane. *The Troubled Crusade: American Education, 1945–1980*. New York: Basic Books, 1983.

Ravitch, Diane, and Chester Finn. *What Do Our 17-Year Olds Know? A Report on the First National Assessment of History and Literature*. New York: Harper & Row, 1987.

Riesman, David. *On Higher Education*. San Francisco: Jossey-Bass, 1980.

Riesman, David, et al. *Academic Values and Mass Education*. Garden City: Doubleday & Co., Inc., 1970.

Rose, Mike. *Lives on the Boundary: The Struggles and Achievements of America's Underprepared*. New York: The Free Press, 1989.

Rose, Mike, ed. *When a Writer Can't Write*. New York: The Guilford Press, 1985.

Rosen, David, Seth Brunner, and Steve Fowler. *Open Admissions: The Promise and the Lie of Open Access to American Higher Education*. Lincoln: University of Nebraska Printing and Duplicating Service, 1976.

Rudolph, Frederick. *Curriculum: A History of the American Under-Graduate Course of Study Since 1636*. Washington: Jossey-Bass, 1977.

Ryder, Randall J., and Michel F. Graves. *Reading and Learning in Content Areas*. New York: John Wiley & Sons, Inc. , 2003.

Sadovnik, Alan R. *Equity and Excellence in Higher Education: The Decline of a Liberal Educational Reform*. New York: Peter Lang Publishing, Inc., 1994.

Sarason, Seymour B. *The Culture of the School and the Problem of Change*. Boston: Allyn and Bacon, Inc., 1979.

Scholes, Robert, and Nancy R. Comley. *The Practice of Writing*. New York: St. Martin's Press, 1981.

Shor, Ira, and Caroline Pari. *Critical Literacy in Action: Writing Words, Changing Worlds*. Portsmouth, NH: Heinemann, 1999.

Spear, Karen I., ed. *Rejuvenating Introductory Courses*. Washington: Jossey-Bass, 1984.

Stam, James, and J. Victor Baldridge. *The Dynamics of Conflict on Campus: A Study of the Stanford April Third Movement*. Stanford: Stanford Center for Research and Development in Teaching, 1971.

Tatum, Beverly D. "Talking about Race, Learning about Racism: The Application of Racial Identity Development Theory in the Classroom." *Harvard Educational Review*, 62 No. 1, Spring 1992.

Taylor, Warner. *A National Survey of Conditions in Freshman English*. Madison, WI: Bureau of Educational Research, 1929.

Tierney, William G. *Curricular Landscapes, Democratic Vistas: Transformative Leadership in Higher Education*. New York: Praeger Publishers, 1989.

Tokarczyk, Michelle M., and E. A. Fay. *Working-Class Women in the Academy*. Amherst: University of Massachusetts Press, 1993.

Traub, James. *City on a Hill*. Reading, MA: Addison-Wesley, 1994.

Whipple, William R. "Collaborative Learning: Recognizing It When We See It," *AAHE Bulletin*, Oct. 1987.

Willie, Charles V., and A. S. McCord. *Black Students at White Colleges*. New York: Praeger, 1972.

Willie, Charles V. *The Sociology of Urban Education*. Lexington, MA: D. C. Heath, 1978.

Willie, Charles V., M. Garibaldi, and W. Reed. *The Education of African-Americans*. New York: Auburn House, 1991.

Witte, Stephen P., and Lester Faigley. *Evaluating College Writing Programs*. Carbondale: Southern Illinois Press, 1983.

Wolf, Maryanne, Mark K. Mcquillan, and Eugene Radwin, eds. *Thought & Language/Language & Reading*. Cambridge: Harvard Educational Review, 1980.

HISTORY OF SCHOOLS & SCHOOLING

THIS SERIES EXPLORES THE HISTORY OF SCHOOLS AND SCHOOLING in the United States and other countries. Books in this series examine the historical development of schools and educational processes, with special emphasis on issues of educational policy, curriculum and pedagogy, as well as issues relating to race, class, gender, and ethnicity. Special emphasis will be placed on the lessons to be learned from the past for contemporary educational reform and policy. Although the series will publish books related to education in the broadest societal and cultural context, it especially seeks books on the history of specific schools and on the lives of educational leaders and school founders.

For additional information about this series or for the submission of manuscripts, please contact the general editors:

Alan R. Sadovnik
Rutgers University-Newark
Education Dept.
155 Conklin Hall
175 University Avenue
Newark, NJ 07102

Susan F. Semel
The City College of New York, CUNY
138th Street and Convent Avenue
NAC 5/208
New York, NY 10031

To order other books in this series, please contact our Customer Service Department:

800-770-LANG (within the U.S.)
212-647-7706 (outside the U.S.)
212-647-7707 FAX

Or browse online by series at:

www.peterlangusa.com